WORLD OF ANIMALS

15

BIRDS

HUNTING BIRDS

Osprey, Bald Eagle, Owls, Nightjars ...

JOHN WOODWARD

GROLIER

Clinton Macomb
Public Library

Owls are mainly night hunters.
Spectacled owl (1); eagle owl (2);
spotted wood owl (3).

Published 2003 by Grolier,
Danbury, CT 06816
An imprint of Scholastic Library Publishing

This edition published exclusively for the school
and library market

Planned and produced by
Andromeda Oxford Limited
Kimber House
1 Kimber Road
Abingdon, Oxon OX14 3PX

www.andromeda.co.uk

Project Director: Graham Bateman
Project Manager: Derek Hall
Editors: Marion Dent, John Woodward
Art Editor and Designer: Tony Truscott
Cartographic Editor: Tim Williams
Editorial Assistants: Marian Dreier,
Rita Demetriou

Picture Manager: Claire Turner
Picture Researcher: Vickie Walters
Production: Clive Sparling

Printed in China

Set ISBN 0-7172-5731-2

Library of Congress Cataloging-in-Publication Data

Birds.
    v. cm. — (World of animals ; v. 11-20)
Includes index.
Contents: [1] Ground birds / Rob A. Hume — [2] Seabirds / Jonathan Elphick — [3] Shorebirds / Derek
W. Niemann, Euan Dunn — [4] Waterbirds / Tony Whitehead, Derek W. Niemann, David Chandler —
[5] Hunting birds / John Woodward — [6] Seed-, fruit-, and nectar-eating birds / Dominic Couzens —
[7] Insectivorous birds / Rob A. Hume — [8] Omnivorous birds / Derek W. Niemann, David Chandler,
Tony Whitehead — [9] Tropical forest birds / Jonathan Elphick — [10] Unusual birds / Dominic
Couzens.
    ISBN 0-7172-5731-2 (set) — ISBN 0-7172-5732-0 (v. 1) — ISBN
0-7172-5733-9 (v. 2) — ISBN 0-7172-5734-7 (v. 3) — ISBN
0-7172-5735-5 (v. 4) — ISBN 0-7172-5736-3 (v. 5) — ISBN
0-7172-5737-1 (v. 6) — ISBN 0-7172-5738-X (v. 7) — ISBN
0-7172-5739-8 (v. 8) — ISBN 0-7172-5740-1 (v. 9) — ISBN
0-7172-5741-X (v. 10)
    1. Birds—Juvenile literature. [1. Birds.] I. Series: World of animals
(Danbury, Conn.) ; v. 11-20.
QL676.2.B57 2003
598—dc21
                                        2003048308

About This Volume

Some of the most fascinating and dramatic of all birds live by hunting other animals. They include huge, powerful eagles like the harpy eagle—a bird that is capable of carrying away a small deer in its massive talons; high-speed hunters of the air like the bird-killing peregrine falcon; and stealth killers such as the night-flying owls. But among the hunting birds there are also aerial insect hunters like the superbly maneuverable swifts and swallows that catch their prey with delicate precision as they soar through the sky, and ground-attack specialists like the rollers and shrikes that often rely on ambush to capture a meal. Although many other birds kill and eat animal prey, the birds described in this volume stand apart for the way in which they demonstrate an intense refinement of the predatory skills of detection, pursuit, and capture. But there is more to these birds than just superb hunting techniques; many have elaborate and unusual lifestyles, and their struggle for survival is no less arduous than it is for other birds. We may marvel at hunting birds, but we have also been their bitter enemies. Millions of hunting birds have been deliberately killed because of the threat they seem to pose to livestock and game. Many more have been poisoned by agricultural pesticides. However, after centuries of persecution many hunting birds are now benefiting from legal protection and are reappearing in the skies to astonish us with their deadly elegance.

Contents

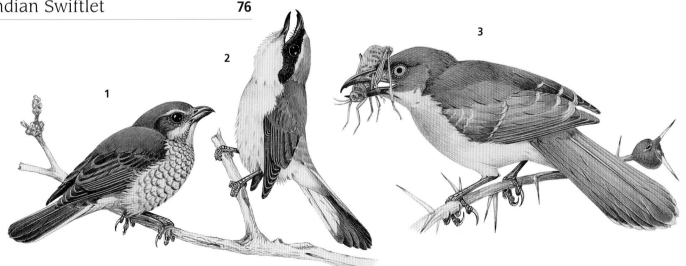

Barn swallows are so aerobatic that they can even feed each other while in flight.

Female red-backed shrike (1) being courted by male (2); gray-headed bush-shrike with grasshopper prey (3).

2

3

1

How to Use This Set

World of Animals: Birds is a 10-volume set that describes in detail birds from all corners of the globe. Each volume brings together those species that share similar characteristics or have similar lifestyles. So birds that spend most of their lives living on the ground are found in Volume 11, seabirds are in volume 12, shorebirds are in Volume 13, and so on. To help you find the volumes containing species that interest you, look at pages 6 to 7 (Find the Animal). A brief introduction to each volume is also given on page 2 (About This Volume).

Data panel presents basic statistics of each bird

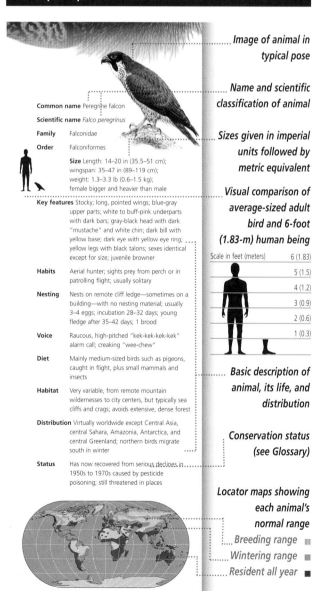

Image of animal in typical pose

Name and scientific classification of animal

Common name	Peregrine falcon
Scientific name	*Falco peregrinus*
Family	Falconidae
Order	Falconiformes
Size	Length: 14–20 in (35.5–51 cm); wingspan: 35–47 in (89–119 cm); weight: 1.3–3.3 lb (0.6–1.5 kg); female bigger and heavier than male
Key features	Stocky; long, pointed wings; blue-gray upper parts; white to buff-pink underparts with dark bars; gray-black head with dark "mustache" and white chin; dark bill with yellow base; dark eye with yellow eye ring; yellow legs with black talons; sexes identical except for size; juvenile browner
Habits	Aerial hunter; sights prey from perch or in patrolling flight; usually solitary
Nesting	Nests on remote cliff ledge—sometimes on a building—with no nesting material; usually 3–4 eggs; incubation 28–32 days; young fledge after 35–42 days; 1 brood
Voice	Raucous, high-pitched "kek-kek-kek-kek" alarm call; creaking "wee-chew"
Diet	Mainly medium-sized birds such as pigeons, caught in flight, plus small mammals and insects
Habitat	Very variable, from remote mountain wildernesses to city centers, but typically sea cliffs and crags; avoids extensive, dense forest
Distribution	Virtually worldwide except Central Asia, central Sahara, Amazonia, Antarctica, and central Greenland; northern birds migrate south in winter
Status	Has now recovered from serious declines in 1950s to 1970s caused by pesticide poisoning; still threatened in places

Sizes given in imperial units followed by metric equivalent

Visual comparison of average-sized adult bird and 6-foot (1.83-m) human being

Scale in feet (meters)
- 6 (1.83)
- 5 (1.5)
- 4 (1.2)
- 3 (0.9)
- 2 (0.6)
- 1 (0.3)

Basic description of animal, its life, and distribution

Conservation status (see Glossary)

Locator maps showing each animal's normal range

- Breeding range
- Wintering range
- Resident all year

Article Styles

Each volume contains two types of article. The first kind introduces individual bird families (such as the penguin family) or groups of closely related bird families (such as mockingbirds and accentors). This article reviews the variety of birds in the families as well as their relationship with other bird families and orders. The second type of article makes up most of each volume. It concentrates on describing in detail individual birds typical of the family or families, such as the blue jay. Each such article starts with a fact-filled **data panel** to help you gather information at a glance. Used together, the two styles of article enable you to become familiar with specific birds in the context of their evolutionary history and biological relationships.

Article describes a particular bird

Scientific name of animal

Common name of animal

Captions to photographs provide additional information about each animal's lifestyle

Cross-references to relevant pages in this and other volumes

Easy-to-read and comprehensive text

A number of other features help you navigate through the volumes and present you with helpful extra information. At the bottom of many pages are **cross-references** to other articles of interest. They may be to related birds, birds that live in similar places, birds with similar behavior, predators (or prey), and much more. Each volume also contains a **Set Index** to the complete *World of Animals: Birds*. All birds mentioned in the text are indexed by common and scientific names, and many topics are also covered. There is also a **Glossary** that will help you if there are words in the text that you do not fully understand. Each volume includes a list of useful **Further Reading and Websites** that help you take your research further. Under **List of Orders and Families** you will find a complete checklist of all the bird families of the world, highlighting the ones that are featured in the set.

Introductory article describes family or closely related groups

Graphic full-color photographs bring text to life

Tables summarize classification of families and give scientific names of animals mentioned in the text. They also list the total number of genera and species in each family

Meticulous drawings illustrate a typical selection of family or group members or supplement text

At-a-glance boxes cover topics of special interest

Find the Animal

*W*orld of Animals: Birds is the second part of a library that describes all groups of living animals. Each cluster of volumes in *World of Animals* will cover a familiar group of animals—mammals, birds, reptiles, amphibians, fish, and insects and other invertebrates. These groups also represent categories of animals recognized by scientists (see The Animal Kingdom below).

The Animal Kingdom

The living world is divided into five kingdoms, one of which (kingdom Animalia) is the main subject of the *World of Animals*. Kingdom Animalia is divided into numerous major groups called phyla, but only one of them (Chordata) contains those animals that have a backbone. Chordates, or vertebrates, include all the animals familiar to us and those most studied by scientists—mammals, birds, reptiles, amphibians, and fish. There are about 38,000 species of vertebrates, while the phyla that contain animals without backbones (so-called invertebrates, such as insects and spiders) include at least 1 million species, probably many more. To find which set of volumes in the *World of Animals* you need to choose, see the chart The Main Groups of Animals (below).

Birds in Particular

World of Animals: Birds provides a broad survey of some of the most abundant yet unusual and varied creatures that share our planet. Birds are unique in their possession of feathers—a feature that allows the majority of species to fly. Birds are divided into major groups called orders.

Rank	Scientific name	Common name
Phylum	Chordata	Animals with a backbone
Class	Aves	All birds
Order	Charadriiformes	Gulls and their relatives
Family	Sternidae	Terns
Genus	*Sterna*	Sea terns
Species	*caspia*	Caspian tern

The kingdom Animalia is subdivided into phyla, classes, orders, families, genera, and species. Above is the classification of the Caspian tern.

Different orders include birds such as birds of prey, owls, and perching birds. Within each order there are a number of bird families. All the bird orders are shown on the chart on page 7; the common names of some of the most important birds in these orders are also listed. For a comprehensive listing of all the bird families within each order refer to the list on pages 112–113.

Bird classification is a rapidly changing science. Not only have several different ways of grouping birds already been proposed, but new evidence, such as from DNA analysis, has resulted in a major rethinking of the bird family tree; the result is that some species are now placed in different orders or families by different ornithologists. Furthermore, the same bird may have a different scientific or common name according to which classification system is used. Therefore, the system of classification in this set may differ in some respects from others and may itself change as the results of new studies emerge.

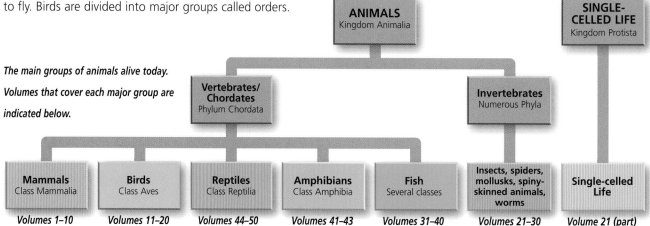

The main groups of animals alive today. Volumes that cover each major group are indicated below.

ANIMALS Kingdom Animalia

SINGLE-CELLED LIFE Kingdom Protista

Vertebrates/ Chordates Phylum Chordata

Invertebrates Numerous Phyla

Mammals Class Mammalia	**Birds** Class Aves	**Reptiles** Class Reptilia	**Amphibians** Class Amphibia	**Fish** Several classes	**Insects, spiders, mollusks, spiny-skinned animals, worms**	**Single-celled Life**
Volumes 1–10	*Volumes 11–20*	*Volumes 44–50*	*Volumes 41–43*	*Volumes 31–40*	*Volumes 21–30*	*Volume 21 (part)*

Naming Birds

To discuss animals, names are needed for the different kinds. Most people regard Caspian terns as one kind of bird and Arctic terns as another. All Caspian terns look alike. They breed together and produce young like themselves. This popular distinction corresponds closely to the zoologists' definition of a species. All Caspian terns belong to one species and all Arctic terns to another.

Some animals have different names in different languages or more than one name in a single language. Therefore, zoologists use an internationally recognized system for naming species consisting of two-word scientific names, usually in Latin or Greek. The Caspian tern is called *Sterna caspia* and the Arctic tern *Sterna paradisaea*. The first word, *Sterna*, is the name of the genus (a group of very similar species), which includes the Caspian tern and the Arctic tern. The second word, *caspia* or *paradisaea*, indicates the species within the genus. The same scientific names are recognized the world over. The convention allows for precision and helps avoid confusion. However, a species may have more than one scientific name—it may have been described and named at different times without the zoologists realizing it was one species.

It is often necessary to make statements about larger groups of animals: for example, all the terns or all the birds. Classification makes this possible. Gulls are similar to terns, but less similar than species are to each other. All gull species are placed in the family Laridae, but all gull-like birds, including the tern family, the Sternidae, are placed in the order Charadriiformes. All the bird orders, each containing birds with similarities to each other, are placed in the class Aves (the birds). Finally, the birds are included, with all other animals that have backbones (fish, amphibians, reptiles, and mammals) and some other animals that seem to be related to them, in the phylum Chordata.

The chart shows the likely relationship between groups of birds, although there is disagreement about some of the links. The volume(s) in which each order appears is also indicated. You can find individual entries by looking at the contents page for each volume or by consulting the index.

Ostrich **Order Struthioniformes** *Volume 11*
Emu, cassowaries **Order Casuariiformes** *Volume 11*
Rheas **Order Rheiformes** *Volume 11*
Kiwis **Order Apterygiformes** *Volume 11*
Tinamous **Order Tinamiformes** *Volume 11*

Game birds **Order Galliformes** *Volume 11*

Wildfowl **Order Anseriformes** *Volume 12, 14*

Button quails **Order Gruiformes** *Volume 11*

Honeyguides, jacamars **Order Piciformes** *Volume 17*
Woodpeckers **Order Piciformes** *Volume 18*
Puffbirds, barbets, toucans **Order Piciformes** *Volume 19*

Kingfishers **Order Coraciiformes** *Volume 14*
Rollers **Order Coraciiformes** *Volume 15*
Bee-eaters, hoopoe **Order Coraciiformes** *Volume 17*
Motmots, todies, hornbills **Order Coraciiformes** *Volume 19*
Trogons **Order Trogoniformes** *Volume 19*

Mousebirds **Order Coliiformes** *Volume 20*

Cuckoos, hoatzin **Order Cuculiformes** *Volume 20*

Parrots **Order Psittaciformes** *Volume 16, 19, 20*

Swifts **Order Apodiformes** *Volume 15*
Hummingbirds **Order Apodiformes** *Volume 16*

Owls **Order Strigiformes** *Volume 15*
Nightjars, frogmouths **Order Caprimulgiformes** *Volume 15*
Turacos **Order Cuculiformes** *Volume 16*

Pigeons **Order Columbiformes** *Volume 16*

Bustards, seriemas **Order Gruiformes** *Volume 11*
Cranes, limpkin, rails **Order Gruiformes** *Volume 14*
Trumpeters **Order Gruiformes** *Volume 19*

Pratincoles, coursers **Order Charadriiformes** *Volume 11*
Gulls, terns, auks **Order Charadriiformes** *Volume 12*
Plovers, sandpipers, avocets, oystercatchers, sheathbills **Order Charadriiformes** *Volume 13*
Jacanas, painted snipes **Order Charadriiformes** *Volume 14*
Sandgrouse **Order Pteroclidiformes** *Volume 16*

Birds of prey **Order Falconiformes** *Volume 15*
Vultures, secretary bird **Order Falconiformes** *Volume 20*

Grebes **Order Podicipediformes** *Volume 14*

Tropicbirds **Order Pelecaniformes** *Volume 12*

Gannets, cormorants **Order Pelecaniformes** *Volume 12*

Herons, storks, ibises, spoonbills, flamingos **Order Ciconiiformes** *Volume 14*
New World vultures **Order Falconiformes** *Volume 20*

Penguins **Order Sphenisciformes** *Volume 12*
Albatrosses, petrels, shearwaters **Order Procellariiformes** *Volume 12*
Pelicans, frigatebirds **Order Pelecaniformes** *Volume 12*
Loons **Order Gaviiformes** *Volume 14*

Perching birds **Order Passeriformes** *Volume 11, 14, 15, 16, 17, 18, 19, 20*

Birds of Prey

Pandionidae, Falconidae, Accipitridae, Cathartidae, Sagittariidae

Family Pandionidae: 1 species

Pandion	osprey (*P. haliaetus*)

Family Falconidae: 10 genera, 57 species, including:

Falco	38 species, including common kestrel (*F. tinnunculus*); northern hobby (*F. subbuteo*); peregrine falcon (*F. peregrinus*); gyrfalcon (*F. rusticolus*); prairie falcon (*F. mexicanus*); lesser kestrel (*F. naumanni*); Mauritius kestrel (*F. punctatus*); merlin (*F. columbarius*)
Micrastur	5 species, including barred forest-falcon (*M. ruficollis*)
Microhierax	1 species, black-legged falconet (*F. fringillarius*)
Polyborus	1 species, crested caracara (*P. plancus*)

Family Accipitridae: 58 genera, 221 species, including:

Accipiter	46 species, including northern sparrowhawk (*A. nisus*); sharp-shinned hawk (*A. striatus*); northern goshawk (*A. gentilis*)
Buteo	26 species, including Eurasian buzzard (*B. buteo*)
Circus	10 species, including hen harrier (*C. cyaneus*)
Aquila	8 species, including golden eagle (*A. chrysaetos*); Verreaux's eagle (*A. verreauxii*)
Haliaeetus	8 species, including bald eagle (*H. leucocephalus*); Steller's sea eagle (*H. pelagicus*)
Pernis	3 species, including honey buzzard (*P. apivorus*)
Milvus	2 species, black kite (*M. migrans*); red kite (*M. milvus*)
Rostrhamus	2 species, including Everglade or snail kite (*R. sociabilis*)
Polemaetus	1 species, martial eagle (*P. bellicosus*)
Elanoides	1 species, swallow-tailed kite (*E. forficatus*)
Harpia	1 species, American harpy eagle (*H. harpyja*)
Oroaetus	1 species, Isidor's eagle (*O. isidori*)
Machaerhamphus	1 species, bat hawk (*M. alcinus*)
Terathopius	1 species, bateleur (*T. ecaudatus*)

Family Cathartidae: 5 genera, 7 species, including:

Vultur	1 species, Andean condor (*V. gryphus*)
Gymnogyps	1 species, California condor (*G. californianus*)

Family Sagittariidae: 1 species

Sagittarius	secretary bird (*S. serpentarius*)

Of all the birds that hunt for their food, birds of prey are the most spectacular. The group includes powerful eagles that swoop from the sky to pluck monkeys from trees, scythe-winged falcons that slice through the air to catch other birds on the wing, and astonishing fishing hawks that plunge headlong into seas and rivers to seize their slippery, struggling victims.

Also known as raptors, birds of prey are found worldwide in every conceivable habitat, apart from the open ocean and the frozen wastes of Antarctica and central Greenland. There are nearly 300 different species, ranging in size from the colossal condors with their 10-foot (3-m) wingspans to tiny pygmy falcons no larger than sparrows. Despite their variety, all birds of prey are instantly recognizable, for they have one obvious feature in common: a wickedly hooked bill. The bill is only rarely used for killing, however. Usually, it is employed for ripping through skin and tearing meat from bones. It is perfectly adapted for the task, allowing even the largest eagles to present their near-helpless nestlings with delicate slivers of meat.

⤒ *Like all birds of prey, the osprey has a large, hooked bill that it uses for tearing into the flesh of its victim. Huge, forward-facing eyes help birds of prey detect their food and then strike with great accuracy.*

 SEE ALSO Osprey **15**:14; Falcon, Peregrine **15**:18; Kestrel, Common **15**:22; Caracara, Crested **15**:24; Kite, Everglade **15**:28

⊕ *Verreaux's eagle, also known as the black eagle, is the African equivalent of the golden eagle. It lives in rocky mountain and savanna habitats and feeds on medium-sized mammals. The bird performs a spectacular diving and swooping display flight during courtship.*

Most birds of prey kill with their powerful feet, which are armed with strong, sharp claws or talons. At the moment of impact the raptor throws its legs forward, squeezing its toes together to impale and crush the life from its victim. Many species, like the merlin, have developed extralong legs to give them an extended reach. Sometimes the legs are thickly feathered for protection. The talons also hold prey securely while it is being carried to the bird's feeding perch or nest.

The other feature that birds of prey have in common is their excellent vision. Like most birds, they are active mainly by day and target their victims by sight. Each eye is huge in comparison with the bird's head—an eagle's eye is bigger than a human's—and packed with sensory cells to see fine detail. Forward-facing eyes provide binocular vision for gauging depth and distances accurately when the bird makes the fatal strike.

Wings for the Job

Different birds of prey have different types of wings to suit their lifestyles. Eagles and buzzards have long, broad wings that are ideal for soaring slowly on updrafts and rising currents of warm air. Their long airfoil-shaped inner sections provide plenty of lift, while the slots between the "fingers" at their wingtips suppress the air turbulence that causes stalling at low speeds. In contrast, fast-flying falcons that hunt birds in the open sky rarely soar, and they have long, pointed wings with long outer flight feathers that give maximum propulsive force and speed.

Low-flying harriers have very large wings relative to their body weight, so they can float slowly over long grass in search of food. But forest hawks need to dart and swerve between trees and branches as they chase their prey, so they have short, rounded wings for maneuverability and long tails for steering.

Social Life

Most hawks and eagles are lone hunters that rely on surprise and speed to catch their quarry. Surprise is often a vital element when catching prey like a bird, reptile, or mammal, because they are alert to the slightest hint of danger. For many big raptors, hunting alone over an exclusive territory is the best way of achieving surprise. A pair of birds may share a territory, but few regularly cooperate to make a kill.

The most extreme example of isolation is probably seen in the martial eagle. Each pair ranges over a vast tract of African savanna grassland, usually covering an area of 60–80 square miles (155–207 sq km). Since they will not tolerate other martial eagles hunting or even roosting on their territory, the species is one of the most thinly distributed in the world.

Birds of prey that hunt less alert prey, such as insects, may hunt together. Small falcons and kites often hunt communally, because they can attack insects and other small creatures without resorting to surprise tactics. The birds often spend the night together in communal roosts, emerging by day to seek out vast swarms of locusts or breeding termites. One roost in tropical Africa was occupied by at least 50,000 small falcons of various species. The snail kites of the American tropics and subtropics live and feed communally in a similar way.

Between these two extremes are found species like the harriers and larger kites—they may spend the night together but scatter during the day. Hen harriers (marsh hawks), for example, gather in groups of ten to fifty birds on winter nights, roosting on platforms of flattened reeds and grasses in marshland. Soon after dawn the roosts break up, and the birds disperse to hunt for birds and other small animals.

Sometimes, even lone hunters come together to feed on unusually rich concentrations of prey. Fish eagles especially abandon their solitary habits to exploit big shoals of fish. For example, the American bald eagle congregates in large numbers to feast on densely packed spawning salmon in Alaskan rivers, and the majestic Steller's sea eagle is famous for the way it gathers to feed off the sea ice of northern Japan in winter. Similarly, a well-stocked garbage dump will often attract eagles, kites, and other raptors on the lookout for easy pickings.

Breeding Strategy

Birds of prey that feed together generally breed together, too. The insect-eating lesser kestrel of southern Eurasia often feeds in flocks, and it also nests in colonies of up to 200 pairs of birds, each pair rearing up to five chicks. Sociable roosters such as harriers and kites may also

⊕ *The Eurasian buzzard is a medium to large hawk that is often seen soaring over its habitat on broad, outstretched wings. Small mammals such as rodents form a major part of its prey, but the bird will also feed on carrion. This buzzard is eating a rabbit.*

SEE ALSO Eagle, Bald **15:**30; Bateleur **15:**36; Goshawk, Northern **15:**38; Eagle, American Harpy **15:**40; Eagle, Golden **15:**44

Back from the Brink

Many birds of prey are rare, but few have hovered so close to the edge of extinction as the Mauritius kestrel. This stocky, short-winged hunter lives only on Mauritius—an island that was the home of the extinct dodo (*Raphus cucullatus*). The Mauritius kestrel was probably never common, but by 1974 deforestation, shooting, pesticide, and egg-thieving monkeys had reduced its entire population to just six birds. They included only two breeding pairs. By an amazing stroke of fortune one of the pairs decided to nest in a hole in a sheer cliff in 1974, rather than in a more usual tree site. The cliff nest was safe from monkeys, and the kestrels managed to raise three chicks—unlike the other pair. When the offspring matured, they also chose to nest on the cliff, and by 1976 they had increased the population to 15 birds.

Eventually, conservationists started breeding the Mauritius kestrels in captivity, and by the late 1980s they were releasing captive-bred birds back into the wild. Today, there are about 800 Mauritius kestrels living on the island, proving that in conservation there is no such thing as a lost cause.

breed in loose colonies, although the nests are more widely spaced, with at least 230 feet (70 m) between them. Up to 49 pairs of black kites have been known to nest in company like this, together with five pairs of the rarer, less gregarious red kites.

Such arrangements are unusual, though, because most raptors breed in isolation. Each pair claims a feeding territory around a suitable nest site—a tall tree, a sheer cliff, or even a ledge on a skyscraper—and the birds monopolize the hunting around it to ensure they can find enough food for their young. Sometimes the territories overlap, but often they are jealously defended.

The bigger the birds, the bigger their territory; so while a pair of forest-hunting sparrowhawks might nest in a wood with an area of only 25 acres (10 ha), a pair of similar but much bigger goshawks needs an area of at least 250 acres (100 ha). This means that a wood that might support ten pairs of breeding sparrowhawks can

support only one pair of goshawks. Very big solitary breeders like eagles need huge territories to themselves. Therefore they space themselves even more widely, and so they are much less common than smaller hawks, even in regions of unspoiled wilderness.

Threats

In many parts of the world there is no such thing as unspoiled wilderness, and the pockets of wild habitat that remain are too small to allow big birds of prey to breed. They may not even be able to find suitable nest sites. The need for space has eliminated big birds of prey from regions where their habitat is being turned into farmland or built on. Big raptors are also very conspicuous, so they make easy targets for hunters, game wardens, or farmers who believe the birds kill their stock.

Smaller species are less vulnerable, but they have suffered badly from the effects of poisonous pesticides ingested by their prey. Many have also died through eating poisoned bait laid out for wolves and foxes. Another threat comes from nest robbing for eggs and nestlings, which are then reared for the falconry trade.

Luckily, many of these threats are receding as more birds of prey enjoy legal protection, and people become more aware of the value of wildlife conservation. But the greatest threat—loss of wild habitat—seems likely to become more acute as human populations grow and their economic expectations increase.

The Osprey

The fish-eating osprey has such a unique combination of features that it is classified in a family of its own, the Pandionidae. Found virtually worldwide wherever there is water to hunt in and suitable sites for breeding, it is one of the most successful of all birds of prey.

Falcons and Caracaras

The family Falconidae includes two groups of birds of prey that have very different lifestyles: the highly predatory falcons and the scavenging caracaras.

Many falcons specialize in aerial attack. For example, the northern hobby chases small birds through the sky at high speed and can even catch a swift. Its larger relative the peregrine has developed an even more spectacular technique, pinpointing its victim from high above and stooping down on half-closed wings to collide with it like a guided missile. The tropical American forest-falcons

It is not surprising that the members of such a large and inclusive family employ a wide variety of hunting techniques. Many hawks and eagles save energy by hunting from perches overlooking open ground—watching and perhaps listening for their victims. In woodland short-winged forest hawks like the sparrowhawk and sharp-shinned hawk perch on branches and wait for small songbirds to fly past, then launch themselves in pursuit, dodging and weaving through the trees with deadly agility.

Others, like the African martial eagle, soar on broad wings, circling on rising air currents to gain height before gliding off across country, searching the ground for a potential meal. By contrast, the harriers hunt like owls, flying low and slow over open grasslands or marshes and pouncing on any animals they find.

Some members of the family are specialists at hunting just one type of

⤊ ⤳ *Representative examples of falcons: gyrfalcon (1); prairie falcon (2); black-legged falconet (3).*

hunt from perches in woodland and have short wings and long tails like those of forest hawks. Some species, like the common kestrel, "perch" in the sky, hovering in one spot as they survey the ground below for prey. Other, smaller falcon species feed almost entirely on insects.

By contrast, the caracaras of South, Central, and southern North America behave more like kites or even vultures, feeding opportunistically on scraps and carrion as well as small animals.

Hawks and Eagles

The great majority of birds of prey are grouped into the family Accipitridae, or accipiters. It includes the eagles, forest hawks, kites, harriers, and buzzards (buteos), as well as the Old World vultures. The New World vultures comprise a separate family, the Cathartidae, and both the vultures and the curious secretary bird are covered in Volume 20 of this series.

⤳ *Representative hawks and eagles: hen harrier (1); swallow-tailed kite and prey (2); Isidor's eagle and prey (3); Steller's sea eagle and prey (4).*

animal. One of the most unusual is the bat hawk of tropical Asia and Africa, which undertakes all its hunting at dawn and dusk when cave-dwelling bats are streaming in and out of their roosts. Uniquely, the bat hawk can pluck bats out of the air and swallow them whole—unlike most hawks that must tear large prey apart before eating it.

⊕ *A female sparrowhawk feeds her chicks. Both sexes share the task of building the nest, which is usually sited about 20 to 50 feet (6–15 m) above ground.*

Several African and Asian eagles specialize in killing snakes, including venomous species like cobras and mambas. The curious honey buzzard is almost as fearless, being an expert at digging out and raiding the nests of bees and wasps, seemingly immune to the stings of the enraged defenders. The Everglade or snail kite of Florida and tropical America specializes in hunting snails.

Although most accipiters have their special hunting techniques, they are surprisingly adaptable and never ignore an easy meal. Some, like the black kite, have turned this into a way of life and scavenge most of their food from garbage dumps and even city streets throughout much of Europe, Asia, and Africa. A black kite will eat virtually any food of animal origin, from live-caught birds and mice to half-eaten kebabs snatched from the hands of people eating in the streets!

4

Common name Osprey

Scientific name *Pandion haliaetus*

Family   Pandionidae

Order   Falconiformes

Size Length: 22–23 in (56–58.5 cm); wingspan: 57–67 in (145–170 cm); weight: 2.6–4.3 lb (1.2–2 kg); female slightly larger than male

Key features Long, narrow wings; dark-brown upper parts and mainly white underparts with dark-speckled breast band; white head with dark-brown stripe through yellow eye; black hooked bill; blue-gray legs; sexes identical; immature paler

Habits   Hunts alone over shallow water; spends much time perched near water

Nesting   Large, isolated nest of sticks and grasses, usually in top of tall tree near water; season varies with region; usually 2–3 eggs; incubation 35–43 days; young fledge after 44–59 days; 1 brood

Voice   Loud yelping call; shrill "pyew-pyew-pyew" during territorial display

Diet   Mainly live fish snatched from just below surface of water, plus a few frogs, snakes, and small birds

Habitat   Coasts, estuaries, rivers, lakes, and swamps

Distribution Breeds virtually worldwide except South America, polar regions, deserts, and much of Africa; breeding birds from North America and northern Eurasia winter in warm-temperate and tropical zones

Status   Badly affected by pesticide poisoning during 1960s and 1970s, but now flourishing throughout most of its range

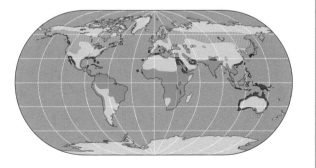

Osprey

Pandion haliaetus

The spectacular hunting style of the fish-catching osprey makes it one of the most recognizable of all birds of prey throughout its huge, almost global range.

THE DISTINCTIVE BROWN-AND-WHITE osprey is a fish hunter. It is so highly specialized that it is classified in a family on its own. Other birds of prey catch fish, but the osprey has acquired a unique combination of adaptations that make it the most widespread and successful of its kind.

The osprey has oily, water-resistant plumage allowing it to plunge underwater to catch its prey, then surface and fly off without difficulty. It can close its nostrils as it dives to prevent water being forced into its lungs. The bird has extremely strong feet to absorb the impact of the dive, reversible outer toes, and long, curved talons. It also has a long, hooked bill as well as a variety of unusual internal features not seen in other birds of prey.

Adaptable Hunter

Ospreys may live in almost any habitat that offers regular supplies of medium-sized fish, from tropical swamps and coastal lagoons to the cold rivers and lakes of the northern forests. They are most numerous in rich, remote coastal habitats such as saltmarshes and mangrove swamps. However, they are unusually tolerant of human activity and are often seen fishing in suburban reservoirs and rivers flowing through

⊕ *The osprey skewers its prey with long, curved talons. The soles of the feet are covered in sharp, spiny scales that help prevent the slippery prize from being dropped while being carried back to the feeding perch.*

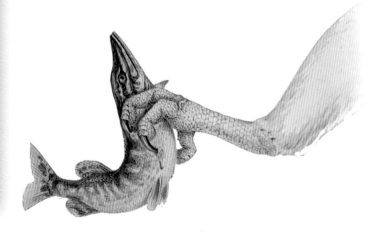

towns. They will even nest in such places, sometimes using man-made nesting platforms provided for the purpose. The willingness to exploit artificial habitats can cause conflicts with humans, however, for they may raid fish farms used for rearing trout or salmon.

Ospreys that breed in the tropics and around the coasts of Australia stay on or near their breeding grounds all year. During the northern winter the tropical residents are joined by birds that have migrated from North America, northern Europe, Scandinavia, Russia, and Siberia. The migrants breed in the north, mainly on the broad rivers and lakes of the great evergreen forests, and then fly south before their feeding waters freeze over. They fly strongly, covering distances of 2,500 to 6,000 miles (4,025–9,650 km). Unlike many birds of

prey, they fly directly toward their destinations without making detours to avoid deserts or deep seas. Therefore, they do not gather in large numbers at favored crossing points like Panama, and it is unusual to see more than one or two ospreys together on migration.

Whether it is on its breeding territory, its wintering grounds, or on migration between the two, an osprey usually hunts in the same way. Cruising some 30–100 feet (9–30 m) above the water, it pauses to hover with its head bent down and legs dangling, searching for a fish just below the surface. If the bird sees a likely prey, it may descend to get a better view before diving headfirst with half-folded wings. Just before the osprey hits the water, it throws its feet forward with talons outspread to seize the fish. Its whole body may disappear

⊕ *An osprey may take almost any medium-sized fish, depending on what is locally available, up to a weight of about 3 pounds (1.4 kg).*

Display Flights

A male osprey usually returns to the breeding site before the female. As soon as he arrives, he stakes his claim with a spectacular switchback display flight, fluttering, wheeling, and diving high over the site, with shrill, whistling calls. When a female arrives, she is attracted by the display and joins him in the performance to strengthen the bond between them.

This type of display flight is common among birds of prey, particularly larger species such as eagles and harriers. In some cases the female flips onto her back in midair so the male can seize her by the talons. Locked together, the pair spiral slowly toward the ground before releasing their grip and flying up again.

underwater with a loud splash, leaving just the wings visible, but it soon struggles free, shakes the water from its feathers, and carries its struggling catch away in its talons, holding it headfirst to reduce wind resistance.

If the fish is too heavy to carry away, the osprey simply drops it, but sometimes the bird's talons are so deeply embedded that it cannot release its grip. Then the weight of the fish may drag its attacker back into the water, and ospreys have been drowned on such occasions.

Big Nests

A typical osprey nest is a big, broad pile of sticks and flotsam lined with soft grass and moss, securely wedged in the crown of a tall tree such as a fir, although the birds will also

nest on cliffs, ruined buildings, artificial platforms, aerials, and even poles supporting electricity lines.

The female usually carries out most of the five-week incubation, while the male keeps her supplied with fish. He also brings food for the chicks when they hatch and keeps the whole family fed until the chicks are fledged. As soon as they can fly, the young ospreys start fishing for themselves, but it takes them weeks, even months, to become as skilled as their parents. Most young ospreys breed in their fourth year.

Brighter Future

Since ospreys build such big, conspicuous nests, they make easy targets for hunters and egg thieves, and in the past they have suffered badly from persecution. As recently as the mid-nineteenth century they bred all over Europe, but within a century shooting and nest destruction had eliminated the breeding populations from nearly all of Europe west of the Black Sea. Then the survivors were hit by a new threat: poisoning by agricultural pesticides.

The worst effects of it were seen in the northeastern U.S., where chemicals draining into waterways and lakes contaminated the fish taken by ospreys as prey. The birds accumulated the poison in their bodies and either died or failed to breed. By the 1970s they were in serious decline; but when the offending chemicals were outlawed in North America and Europe, the situation began to improve. Today osprey populations are recovering strongly in the U.S., and they are also doing well in northern Europe, thanks partly to birds being reintroduced to regions where they were once common. In Scotland, for example, ospreys became extinct in 1902, but a reintroduction plan has now created a viable breeding population of more than 80 pairs.

⊛ *Each pair of ospreys returns to the same site year after year, renovating the old nest and adding more material, so it grows bigger and bigger. Eventually the nest can become so huge that it collapses, and the birds have to begin again on a new site.*

Mated for Life

Like many large birds of prey, ospreys often stay faithful to their partners for life. At the end of the breeding season the birds leave the nest and go their separate ways. When the time comes to mate again, the ospreys instinctively return to the same area. Unless one of the original pair has died, they both come back to the isolated nest, get reacquainted, and start another family.

However, some birds returning to the breeding area have never mated before. If one of a pair fails to arrive, the survivor may mate with one of the unattached birds and rear a brood of chicks in the old nest. If neither of the original breeders returns, a new pair may take over the nest, repair it, and use it themselves for the next few years. The same nest may be reoccupied every year for decades or even centuries.

⊛ *A juvenile osprey calling. The pale undersides act as camouflage to help the bird conceal itself from prey as it swoops over the surface of the water.*

Peregrine Falcon

Falco peregrinus

Common name Peregrine falcon

Scientific name *Falco peregrinus*

Family Falconidae

Order Falconiformes

Size Length: 14–20 in (35.5–51 cm); wingspan: 35–47 in (89–119 cm); weight: 1.3–3.3 lb (0.6–1.5 kg); female bigger and heavier than male

Key features Stocky; long, pointed wings; blue-gray upper parts; white to buff-pink underparts with dark bars; gray-black head with dark "mustache" and white chin; dark bill with yellow base; dark eye with yellow eye ring; yellow legs with black talons; sexes identical except for size; juvenile browner

Habits Aerial hunter; sights prey from perch or in patrolling flight; usually solitary

Nesting Nests on remote cliff ledge—sometimes on a building—with no nesting material; usually 3–4 eggs; incubation 28–32 days; young fledge after 35–42 days; 1 brood

Voice Raucous, high-pitched "kek-kek-kek-kek" alarm call; creaking "wee-chew"

Diet Mainly medium-sized birds such as pigeons, caught in flight, plus small mammals and insects

Habitat Very variable, from remote mountain wildernesses to city centers, but typically sea cliffs and crags; avoids extensive, dense forest

Distribution Virtually worldwide except Central Asia, central Sahara, Amazonia, Antarctica, and central Greenland; northern birds migrate south in winter

Status Has now recovered from serious declines in 1950s to 1970s caused by pesticide poisoning; still threatened in places

The peregrine is probably the fastest hunter on Earth, capable of launching an airborne attack on its prey at speeds of over 100 miles per hour (160 km/h).

BIG, BURLY, AND AMAZINGLY FAST, the bird-killing peregrine falcon could claim to be the ultimate airborne hunter. It is certainly the most spectacular, likely to attack apparently out of nowhere and strike its prey dead in midair. It must be a strategy for success, because of all birds of prey it is the species that has spread most widely around the globe.

Deadly Hunter

Like nearly all falcons, the peregrine is built for speed. It has sharp-pointed wings adapted for maximum thrust, and they are powered by huge flight muscles that give the bird a heavy, broad-chested look as it perches watching for potential prey. In the air the peregrine is agile and fast, and it has the stamina to cross oceans on its long migration flights. Where there are no suitable vantage points, the bird often searches for prey by circling high in the sky, using its excellent eyesight to pick out a victim below. Once it has a target in view, it may mount an attack that, for sheer speed, has no equal in the natural world.

Already moving fast, the falcon powers into a headfirst dive, or stoop. It may fall almost vertically out of the sky, accelerating all the time

⤸ Peregrines may pass food to each other in flight. Here a female turns on her back to receive a blackbird (Turdus vulgaris) from her mate.

⬅ A peregrine attacking an American bittern (Botaurus lentiginosus). Although peregrines do not usually attack such large prey, they have been known to take birds as big as geese.

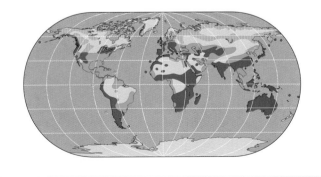

SEE ALSO Bittern, American **14**:30; Birds of Prey **15**:8; Pigeon Family, The **16**:12; American Blackbird Family, The **18**:74

with the air roaring over the feathers of its half-closed wings. Special structures in the bird's airways prevent the rising air pressure bursting its lungs. The bird keeps its eyes open to ensure it stays on target. As the peregrine closes on its victim, it reaches out with its talons, extending a powerful hind claw to slice into its quarry like a can opener. It usually aims for the head, and the high-velocity impact is often enough to kill the victim outright, so it tumbles from the sky in a flurry of bloodstained feathers.

It is a devastating technique but not infallible. The peregrine stoops at such high speed that it cannot easily alter course; and if the intended victim manages to dodge aside at the last moment, the falcon may miss. In fact, many attacks fail at the first attempt, but a peregrine does not give up easily. Swooping around, it may try again, this time relying on active flying speed to overhaul its prey. Often it succeeds—few birds can fly faster than a peregrine, which can achieve 50 miles per hour (80 km/h) in level flight. Occasionally a hunted bird manages to escape by diving into a swirling flock of birds or simply by dropping to the ground and into cover.

Sometimes a bird is not killed by the first strike, so the peregrine has to finish it off with a lethal neck bite. Like all falcons—but not other birds of prey—it has an extra notch in its bill to help it cut through neck bones to sever the spinal cord. Then it either eats the bird where it fell or carries it to a favorite feeding perch, using its hooked bill to rip away feathers and skin to get at the flesh.

The peregrine's main victims are pigeons, crows, ducks, seabirds, or big waders; but it also takes smaller songbirds such as larks and thrushes, plus the occasional insect or small

⊕ A peregrine searches the sky and the ground below for prey. Often the bird simply perches on a suitable lookout post or branch until a likely victim is sighted.

The Falconer's Choice

As the most spectacular hunter among the falcons, the peregrine has traditionally been the bird of choice for falconry. This ancient sport has been practiced for at least 4,000 years, and it is still extremely popular, with as many as 20,000 falconers worldwide.

The birds used for falconry are usually well cared for; and since they are flown free, they have the opportunity to escape if they wish. Yet falconry has a downside. It creates a demand for young peregrines and other falcons. While many are captive-bred, there is a flourishing trade in birds taken from the wild as eggs or nestlings. That is illegal, but nest robbers are prepared to risk fines or imprisonment because they can get a huge sum for every bird they sell. This is a big problem in southern Europe, where many peregrine pairs have their young stolen each year.

① A peregrine stands over its prey with arched wings before eating it. This is known as mantling. The peregrine normally ignores the wings and feet of its victim but strips everything else down to the bone.

mammal picked off the ground. The bigger female takes heavier prey than the male, and that may help a mated pair divide the spoils on their joint territory.

Rich Pickings

During the breeding season peregrines need more food, both for themselves and for their young, and many head north to prey on the huge flocks of waders and wildfowl that breed on the arctic tundra. Like all peregrines, these northern breeders prefer to nest on cliffs and crags; but where suitable nest sites are scarce, they lay their eggs in bare scrapes on the ground. Here they are vulnerable to nest robbers like Arctic foxes, so the birds must be particularly vigilant to drive away any intruders. Other breeding birds suffer in the same way, and in the Siberian Arctic rare red-breasted geese (*Branta ruficollis*) often nest near the peregrines to take advantage of their air defenses. Clearly the risk from the foxes outweighs the risk from the falcons!

Farther south, breeding peregrines favor sea cliffs near seabird nesting colonies or upland wildernesses used as breeding grounds by waders. But some peregrines regularly nest on city towers, chimneys, and bridges. In early spring the pairs perform noisy aerial displays over their nest sites, spiraling into the sky and plummeting down again, sometimes rolling over and clasping talons as they tumble earthward. The male keeps his mate supplied with food as she incubates the eggs and broods the young, but the female also starts hunting when the young are a month old. Most young birds breed in their third year.

At the end of the breeding season northern peregrines move south to warmer regions. Birds that breed in the Canadian Arctic fly all the way to Argentina and Chile, while those from northern Europe and Siberia spend the northern winter in Africa, southern Asia, and Indonesia. Peregrines breeding in milder climates may not travel so far, but in western Europe many leave their nesting sites to hunt over estuaries teeming with waders and wildfowl that have moved south from the Arctic for the winter.

Poisoned

In 1942 mass production of an insecticide called DDT began. The insecticide was effective and inexpensive, and by the 1950s DDT and other "organochlorine" insecticides were being widely used to combat crop pests. Seeds were laced with the chemicals to kill the insects that fed on them, and crop yields soared.

Yet there was a problem brewing for wildlife. Organochlorines take a long time to break down and become harmless. Pigeons and other seed-eating birds started accumulating them in their body fat. When the chemicals washed off the land into waterways, they also entered the bodies of fish. At first the effects went unnoticed. A pigeon might accumulate the DDT from 1,000 seeds and show no side effects. But the poison stays in its body. If a peregrine catches and eats 100 such pigeons, it accumulates the DDT from 100,000 seeds, with disastrous results.

In fact, the main effect of DDT on peregrines was to make their eggshells thinner, so they broke as the birds tried to incubate them. Fish-eating birds of prey like the osprey (*Pandion haliaetus*) and bald eagle (*Haliaeetus leucocephalus*) suffered in the same way. They were also killed outright by stronger organochlorines such as dieldrin and aldrin. So, by destroying both the birds of prey and their eggs, the pesticides threatened to wipe them out altogether.

By the 1970s the problem was recognized, and organochlorine pesticides were virtually banned in North America and Europe. Yet they are still used in the tropics to fight insect-borne diseases like malaria. So although many birds of prey are recovering in the north, pesticide poisoning is still a major threat to their survival.

Victim of War

Like most birds of prey, the peregrine has suffered badly from persecution. Many were shot in the past because they were considered a danger to valuable game birds, and during World War II the peregrines of southern Britain were virtually annihilated because of the threat they posed to homing pigeons carrying messages from occupied Europe.

More recently, huge numbers of peregrines shared the same fate as the osprey, wiped out by pesticide poisoning during the 1960s and 1970s. The entire peregrine population of the eastern U.S. was destroyed by pesticides, plus about 85 percent of the peregrines in the western U.S. The situation in Europe was almost as bad.

The most destructive chemicals are no longer used in North America and Europe, and now many populations of peregrines have completely recovered, thanks partly to birds being bred in captivity and released in areas where they once lived wild. And since peregrines are amazingly adaptable, being prepared to breed almost anywhere, their global future is probably secure.

⊕ *An adult peregrine offers its chick a mouthful of food. The nest has been built among rocks by a river in the Russian Arctic.*

Common name Common kestrel (Eurasian kestrel)

Scientific name *Falco tinnunculus*

Family   Falconidae

Order   Falconiformes

Size Length: 13–15 in (33–38 cm); wingspan: 26–32 in (66–81cm); weight: 5–11 oz (142–312 g); female bigger and heavier than male

Key features Slender, long-tailed, with long, pointed wings; male has blue-gray head and upper tail, chestnut back and wings, and darker flight feathers; female has brown head and tail, duller brown back and wings, barred black; both whitish to buff below, streaked black; dark eye; yellow eye ring, bill base, and legs; juvenile like female

Habits   Usually seen alone, hovering or hunting from a perch

Nesting   In tree cavity, on cliff ledge, or building, or in old crow's nest; season varies with region; 4–6 eggs; incubation 27–31 days; young fledge after 27–35 days; 1 brood

Voice   High, nasal "keee-keee-keee"

Diet   Mainly small mammals, especially voles; also small songbirds, insects, and earthworms

Habitat   Grassland, farmland, open woodland, towns, and roadsides

Distribution Throughout Europe, Scandinavia, most of Asia except the far north, and Africa apart from Sahara; Scandinavian and northern Asian birds migrate south for the winter

Status   Common throughout most of range

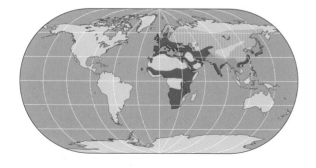

Common Kestrel

Falco tinnunculus

Instantly identifiable by its habit of hovering over roadsides watching for prey on the ground, the kestrel has learned how to exploit a changing world.

FEW BIRDS OF PREY BETRAY their identity as readily as the kestrel. As it flies from its perch across a field, using short, shallow wingbeats punctuated by glides, it could be any small, sharp-winged falcon. But then it pauses in midair, turns and hovers head-on to the wind with quivering wings and flared tail, watching the ground intently. It may drop down to snatch a meal or peel away to search elsewhere, but that masterful hover has given it away.

Roadside Hunter

Over much of Europe the kestrel is the most common and distinctive bird of prey. Its main prey are voles—small rodents that feed in long grass and low vegetation. The kestrel is an expert at detecting voles, either by hunting from a low perch or by hovering some 30 feet (9 m) above the ground. On hillsides the kestrel often hangs in updrafts with scarcely a wingbeat, making constant adjustments with its

⊕ *The kestrel is often a common sight over roadsides, particularly the broad, virtually wild edges of high-speed highways, where it is hard to miss as it hovers almost stationary above the traffic.*

wings and tail to keep its head in exactly the same spot. If the bird detects a movement, it often descends in stages to check it out before making a final plunge on half-closed wings to seize its victim in its talons.

Where voles are scarce, a kestrel may eat insects, mainly beetles snatched from the ground. It also ambushes small birds in the air, but it is no high-speed bird hunter. The kestrel's speciality is steady, detailed searching—and judging by its widespread distribution, the method is very successful.

Unfussy Nesters

Like other falcons, the kestrel does not build a true nest, although it may take over an abandoned nest built by another bird. Otherwise, it selects a tree hole or a ledge or crevice in a rock face or building. Nesting kestrels are common in towns, where they feed mainly on small birds.

The male hunts for the female while she incubates the eggs, and he brings food for both her and the chicks while they are too young to be left alone. His performance as a provider is critical to the chicks' survival. If he cannot bring enough food, the adults may abandon the whole brood. In northern regions, where vole numbers fluctuate in a "boom and bust" cycle, the breeding success of the local kestrels tends to follow the same pattern; more young kestrels are reared in a year in which voles are also plentiful. Most young kestrels first breed in their second year.

Northern kestrels migrate south for the winter. Many fly all the way from Russia to the wooded grasslands of tropical Africa, crossing the Sahara to get there, while others travel to India and Indochina. But many do not migrate so far, and Scandinavian kestrels often spend the winter in the milder climate of Britain. The kestrels that breed further south do not need to migrate to survive the winter, so many remain, although many upland birds move to the lowlands to escape the severest weather.

Poisonous Prey

Like other birds of prey, kestrels have suffered from loss of habitat and pesticide poisoning. They have not been as badly affected as some, though. Their preferred prey—voles—do not accumulate poisons at the same rate as seed-eating birds; so although kestrels declined in the north during the DDT-ravaged 1960s, they did not suffer as badly as bird killers like the peregrine falcon (*Falco peregrinus*) or the northern sparrowhawk (*Accipiter nisus*).

⤋ A field mouse makes a meal for a female common kestrel. The birds can usually find plenty to eat on farmland and in built-up areas, and they are quite prepared to hunt in places where there is lots of human activity.

Common name Crested caracara

Scientific name *Polyborus plancus*

Family	Falconidae
Order	Falconiformes

Size Length: 19–23 in (48–58.5 cm); wingspan: 47–52 in (119–132 cm); weight: 1.8–3.5 lb (0.8–1.6 kg)

Key features Large bird with black cap and crest; powerful bill and bare red face; white throat and neck, barred with black toward breast; brown-black wings and back, with white patch on primary flight feathers; black-barred white tail with black tip; long yellow legs with black feathering; sexes identical; immature browner, with duller bare parts

Habits Often perches or forages on the ground with other scavengers such as vultures

Nesting Large stick nest, usually in a tree; season varies with latitude; 2–3 eggs, rarely 4; incubation 28–32 days; young fledge after 60–80 days; 1, rarely 2, broods

Voice Raucous territorial calls; clicks and grumbles when disturbed at nest

Diet Opportunist hunter and scavenger; prey ranges from fly maggots to live lambs; also eats carcasses, garbage, and plant matter

Habitat Grasslands and semideserts; also marshes and open forests

Distribution Caribbean, southwestern U.S., Central and South America south to Tierra del Fuego

Status Common, despite local persecution

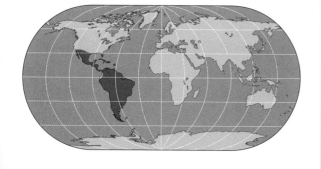

Crested Caracara

Polyborus plancus

Although it looks and behaves like a vulture, the bulky, bare-faced, rather clumsy caracara is actually a close relative of high-speed falcons like the peregrine.

MANY HUNTING BIRDS ARE SPECIALISTS; they have perfected a particular style of hunting and target one type of prey. Others have a different feeding strategy; they use a variety of hunting techniques and will make a meal out of just about anything. That allows them to live in a variety of habitats and to survive environmental changes that would be fatal to a specialist. The adaptable and enterprising crested caracara falls into the latter category.

It lives in open country in Florida, the Caribbean islands, and all over Latin America, from the cactus deserts of Mexico to the windswept wastes of Patagonia. It is most common in lowland areas, but also occurs in the Andes, where pairs have been known to nest at altitudes of up to 10,000 feet (3,050 m). Thriving in such a huge range of climates and habitats requires the ability to take advantage of any opportunities, and the crested caracara is well equipped to exploit all kinds of conditions.

Often First to Arrive

From a distance the crested caracara looks like a long-legged eagle. It has a similar stocky body and broad, rather rounded wings, quite unlike those of its falcon relatives. The caracara often competes for carrion with the more powerful turkey vultures (*Cathartes aura*) and even giant condors (genera *Vultur* and *Gymnogyps*). If the caracara arrives at a carcass after them, it must usually wait its turn, but quite often it is first on the scene. Unlike vultures, the caracara does not soar on rising currents of warm air, but relies instead on its rather slow but active flight. This means it can get into the air at first light, instead of waiting for the Sun to warm the

⊖ *Close up, the caracara is somewhat vulturelike, with a deep, powerful bill and a naked red-skinned face. As with vultures, this naked face is an adaptation for feeding on carrion, allowing the caracara to dig deep into the carcass of an animal without its feathers getting matted with blood.*

ground and create thermal upcurrents. It makes the most of this by mounting a dawn patrol for roadkill and other night-time casualties, so it can get to them before the vultures. It also visits town dumps to pick over the garbage for anything edible.

Yet the crested caracara is not restricted to scavenging. It hunts, too, taking a variety of animals, including slow-flying birds, small mammals, lizards, snakes, fish, crabs, and insects. It waits for turtles to lay their eggs and then uses its flattened claws to dig them up again. The bird also digs beneath dried cowpats for dung beetles. When it arrives at a decomposing carcass, it is often more interested in the fly maggots infesting it than the rotting meat itself.

Caracaras often forage together in small groups, occasionally cooperating to make a kill. They spend a lot of their time on the ground, probing in the undergrowth for tasty morsels or wading in shallow water searching for frogs or dead fish. They also work their way through

Caracaras are quick to spot any dead or injured animals that might make easy prey. They are also big enough to make off with a weak or disabled lamb, and that has earned caracaras a reputation as sheep killers. They are also pirates, stealing food from other caracaras, vultures, gulls, and pelicans.

Pirate Bird

When it comes to finding a meal, the crested caracara will stop at nothing, even theft. Where other birds such as pelicans (genus *Pelecanus*) are feeding successfully and the caracara cannot share their meal, it selects a pelican and harasses the victim until it disgorges the food it has just eaten. The thief makes off with its loot, and the pelican must go fishing again.

Since it steals from the pelican and gives nothing in return, the caracara is behaving as a kind of parasite known as a kleptoparasite. It is not the only bird to act like this. American turkey vultures have been seen bullying young herons into giving up their last meal so the vultures can feed it to their own chicks. It is particularly common among seabirds such as skuas (genus *Catharacta*) and frigatebirds (genus *Fregata*), which often become so expert at securing food by stealing that they give up hunting for their own prey altogether.

 SEE ALSO Pelicans and Their Relatives **12**:44; Frigatebird, Magnificent **12**:62; Gull, Herring **12**:78; Skua, Great **12**:92

⊖ *The crested caracara throws its head back when making its loud territorial calls.*

trees and bushes, raiding the nests of other birds for eggs and nestlings. They will even eat the flesh of coconuts and floating water plants.

Keen Nest Builder

Unlike its falcon relatives, the crested caracara lays its eggs in a specially built nest in the tangled crown of a tree or a big, spiny cactus. If that is not possible, the bird builds the nest in a rock crevice or even on the ground. Many nests are reused year after year and renovated with extra sticks so they grow bigger each season. Both adults incubate the eggs and care for the young, unlike most birds of prey. They must remain at the task for some time because young crested caracaras may take up to three months to grow their flight feathers and leave the nest.

⊖ *Crested caracaras use trees both as vantage points from which to spot food and as nesting sites.*

Weeding Out the Weaklings

Many crested caracaras are shot because they kill lambs and young goats. In reality, however, they probably kill only those that are diseased or crippled and likely to die anyway. All birds of prey are experts at targeting the weak and sick, and rarely waste energy chasing big, healthy quarry.

This means that hunting birds actually benefit the wild animal populations that they prey on by weeding out the weakest individuals. Only the ones that escape get the chance to breed; and since their young tend to inherit their strengths, the population becomes generally healthier. The same thing occurs among caribou and reindeer herds in wolf territory: They are actually fitter than herds that live in regions where the wolves have been wiped out.

Mixed Fortunes

In sheep-rearing regions like southern Argentina the caracara's lamb-killing reputation causes many ranchers to shoot it or poison it with strychnine. In about 1900 one local race that lived on Guadalupe Island off Baja California was shot out of existence by farmers who saw it as a threat to their herds of Angora goats.

Elsewhere it is generally tolerated as a rather useful scavenger. In Mexico, where it is sometimes known as the Mexican eagle, it is legally protected as the country's national bird. Unusually, it seems to be profiting from human changes in the landscape. It is better adapted to open country, so the felling of forests to create grazing land for cattle suits it very well, and its numbers are probably increasing.

Common name Everglade kite (snail kite)

Scientific name *Rostrhamus sociabilis*
(Florida race: *R.s. plumbeus*)

Family Accipitridae

Order Falconiformes

Size Length: 16–18 in (41–46 cm);
wingspan: 45 in (114 cm);
weight: 13–14 oz (369–397 g)

Key features Slim and broad-winged; very slender, long-
hooked bill and red eye; male slate-gray with
black wingtips and white on tail, bare red
skin on face, and red legs; female brown with
paler streaked underparts, orange skin on
face and legs; immature resembles female,
but has brown eye

Habits Very sociable, roosting and feeding together

Nesting Nests in loose colonies; builds stick nests in
reed beds, bushes, or trees; season varies
with latitude; usually 2–4 eggs; incubation
26–28 days; young fledge after 40–49 days,
but may leave nest earlier; 1–3 broods

Voice Bleating cry during courtship display

Diet Normally freshwater apple snails of the genus
Pomacea; also crabs and mice when snails are
scarce

Habitat Marshes

Distribution Florida Everglades, Cuba, southeast Central
America, South America east of Andes

Status Rare, local, and vulnerable in Florida;
common and widespread elsewhere

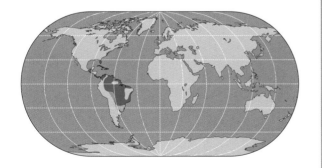

Everglade Kite

Rostrhamus sociabilis

Although it hovers on the edge of extinction in the swamps of Florida, the snail-eating Everglade kite is flourishing throughout most of Latin America.

THE EVERGLADE KITE FEEDS ALMOST exclusively on freshwater snails. This may seem an unusual diet for a bird of prey, but it has several advantages. Snails are very nourishing, being the freshwater equivalent of the shellfish that support vast flocks of wading birds on ocean shores. Snails often occur in huge numbers, allowing many birds to feed together. They are certainly easy to catch, and they never put up a fight. The only problem is getting into them.

The Everglade kite is equipped for the task with a slender bill ending in a very long hook like a curved blade. A captured apple snail usually retreats into its shell and seals itself in with a horny "door" called an operculum, but the kite's bill is slim enough to be slipped between the operculum and the shell. The bird feels for the muscle anchoring the snail inside its shell, slices through it, shakes the snail from its shell, and then gulps it down.

The kite usually hunts from a perch, swooping down to snatch each snail from the shallows with one foot before taking it back to the perch for extraction.

Swamp Dweller

The bird is widespread over the marshy lowlands of tropical America, where it is known as the snail kite. A local race lives in the Everglades of Florida and the swamps of Cuba, and it is called the Everglade kite. The bird relies on a steady supply of *Pomacea* apple snails, and they occur only in the shallow waters of near-permanently flooded marshes and swamps. But where conditions are right, the snails can be found in their millions, supporting large populations of kites. In the Pantanal of southern Brazil, for example, groups of up to 600 kites can be seen foraging together, flying low over the marshes or perched nearby.

If there are no convenient perches from which to hunt, the birds may quarter the marsh with a slow, flapping flight. The kites target the snails visually, so where the water is overgrown with floating vegetation such as water hyacinth—a common plant in the Everglades—the snails cannot be seen, and the birds must look elsewhere. Conversely, a stretch of clear water teeming with snails can attract so many kites that each must defend its feeding patch.

The kites normally spend most of the day looking for snails, then retreat to communal roosts to spend the night. The roosts are often in dense reed beds or on wooded islands in the swamp. In the tropics a single roost may be used by 1,000 or more birds for a season or two before they are forced to move on by changing flood patterns in the marshlands. For a snail kite home is where the snails are.

Sociable Nesters

Everglade kites often breed on their roosting sites, nesting in colonies of up to 100 pairs. Each pair raises two or three chicks; but when snails are abundant, either the male or the female may desert the nest to raise a new family with another bird. Meanwhile, the abandoned bird raises the original brood on its own. Most young Everglade kites breed in their second year.

Throughout much of tropical America snail kites are very common, and in some wetland regions they outnumber all other birds of prey. In the Florida Everglades, however, the species is on the northern edge of its range and struggles to survive. The birds have also suffered badly from droughts, drainage projects, and development destroying their swampland habitat. In the mid-1960s there were only about 50 birds left. Since then careful management of water levels in selected areas has enabled the population to increase to about 500, split between three main areas. Nevertheless, in the Florida Everglades the Everglade kite remains a rare bird.

↑ *The sharp, extralong hook on the Everglade kite's bill is the ideal tool for extracting snails from their shell.*

Common name Bald eagle

Scientific name *Haliaeetus leucocephalus*

Family Accipitridae

Order Falconiformes

Size Length: 28–38 in (71–96.5 cm); wingspan: 66–96 in (168–244 cm); weight: 6.6–13.9 lb (3–6.3 kg); female larger than male; northern race *washingtoniensis* larger than southern race *leucocephalus*

Key features Large eagle with powerful yellow bill; yellow eyes and legs; white head and tail; dark-brown body and wings; sexes identical except for size; juvenile mottled white with dark bill and eye

Habits Normally seen singly or in pairs, but gathers in larger numbers to exploit rich food sources

Nesting Large stick nest, usually in a conifer tree or on a cliff 30–60 ft (9–18 m) above the ground; reused and added to each year; nests in summer in north, winter in south; usually 2 eggs; incubation 34–36 days; young fledge after 70–92 days; 1 brood

Voice A squeaky cackle

Diet Mainly fish; also ducks, rabbits, rodents, turtles, snakes, and carrion

Habitat Usually near open water in all kinds of terrain ranging from cold conifer forest to hot deserts

Distribution Most of North America from southern Alaska and Canada to northern Mexico, plus Aleutian Islands

Status Badly hit by persecution and pesticide poisoning in the past but now flourishing, especially in far northwest of range

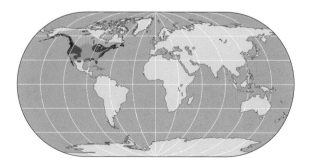

Bald Eagle *Haliaeetus leucocephalus*

Despite being adopted as the national bird of the U.S. in 1782, the magnificent bald eagle has been lucky to survive extinction through the combined effects of shooting, poisoning, and habitat loss.

WITH ITS PIERCING YELLOW EYE, big hooked bill, and fearsome talons, the bald eagle is one of the most imposing of all hunting birds. The name "bald" is misleading, because it suggests a head devoid of feathers like that of a vulture. In fact, the eagle has beautiful snowy white plumage on its head, matching its tail and contrasting with the rich, dark-chocolate plumage of the rest of its body.

The bald eagle is one of eight fish eagles of the genus *Haliaeetus* that includes the white-tailed sea eagle (*H. albicilla*) of Eurasia and the colossal Steller's sea eagle (*H. pelagicus*) of eastern Siberia and Japan. Many of these eagles hunt mainly at sea, but the bald eagle lives all over North America, often far from any ocean. It certainly likes fish, however, and away from coasts it is usually found near the shores of large lakes or by big rivers.

Two Races

There are two distinct races of the bald eagle: the northern and the southern. The northern birds are bigger, and in the summer they breed among the lakes and forests of Canada and

⊕ *An adult (right) and three immature bald eagles scavenging from a garbage dump—the birds are adaptable and inventive feeders, exploiting a variety of food sources.*

 SEE ALSO Birds of Prey **15**:8; Osprey **15**:14; Falcon, Peregrine **15**:18; Vulture, Turkey **20**:12

⊕ When a bald eagle sees a big fish near the water surface, it swoops down, gaffs the fish with its talons, and flies off with it. Bald eagles hardly ever plunge into the water like ospreys, and they usually manage to lift their prey without getting anything other than their feet wet.

Alaska, as far north as the arctic tundra. When the northern rivers and lakes freeze over, many fly south as far as California, Arizona, or Florida. There they usually gather around rivers, lakes, and reservoirs. However, some may spend the winter far from water in dry sagebrush country or even desert, returning to their northern breeding grounds in spring.

Along the Pacific coasts and islands of Alaska and British Columbia the eagles can still feed in the sea even when lakes and rivers freeze, so they stay all year around. Most of the 100,000 or so bald eagles in North America live in this region, which is rich in fish and still largely wilderness.

The smaller, far less numerous southern race breeds in the winter in California, Texas, Louisiana, Florida, and the southern Atlantic states such as Georgia. Many young birds from the south move north toward Canada for the summer, but

other individuals, mainly older adults, stay in the steamy south all summer.

Very Varied Tastes

Bald eagles eat a wide variety of food, dead or alive, depending on the season and availability. Many breeding pairs in the southern states feed their young almost entirely on roadkills—opossums being a favorite—while Alaskan birds scavenging on the seashore may make an outsized meal of a stranded whale.

Live prey is just as important, however, and bald eagles spend a lot of time hunting fish. The eagle is equipped for the task with a pair of massive, long-clawed feet. The toes are short and strong for maximum gripping power, and the hind toe has an extralong, supersharp claw that pierces the fish's body like a dagger and often kills it almost instantly.

Often, the bald

⊕ *Most of the 100,000 or so bald eagles in North America live along the Pacific coasts and islands of Alaska and British Columbia. The area is rich in fish and still largely an unspolied wilderness.*

eagle watches from a perch such as a cliff ledge or a branch before swooping down to the water. Occasionally, bald eagles search for live fish in flight, but hunting from a perch saves energy. They also steal fish from other birds of prey such as ospreys (*Pandion haliaetus*), and a bald eagle may even snatch a meal from a sea otter as it floats on its back among the seaweed, gnawing at a fish held between its front paws.

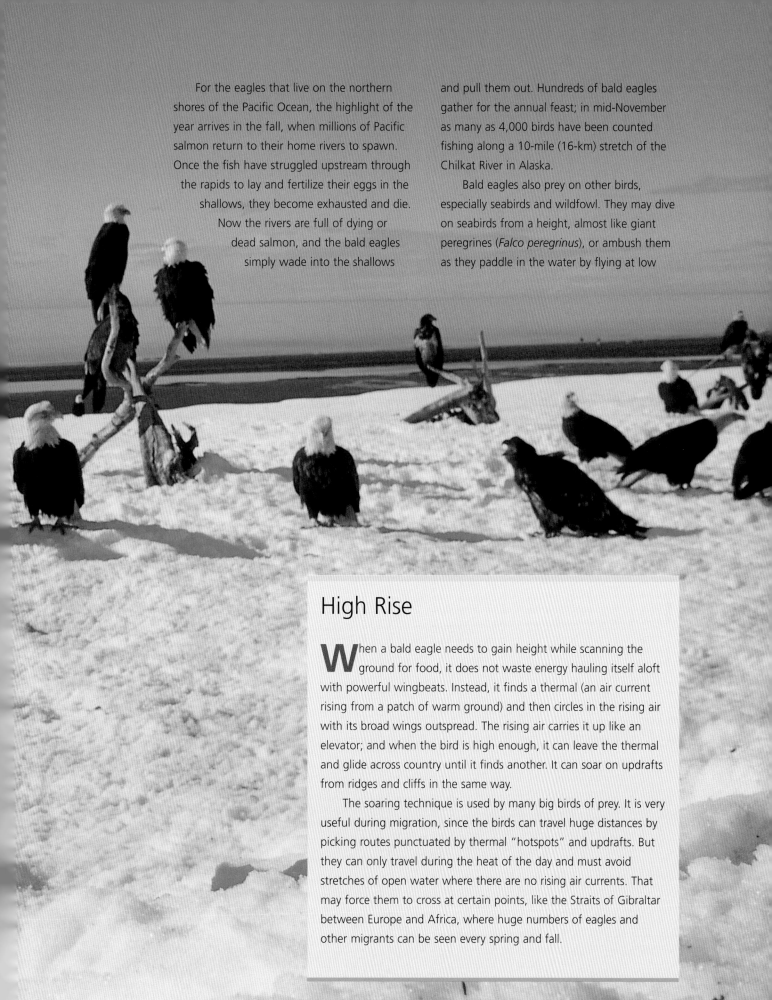

For the eagles that live on the northern shores of the Pacific Ocean, the highlight of the year arrives in the fall, when millions of Pacific salmon return to their home rivers to spawn. Once the fish have struggled upstream through the rapids to lay and fertilize their eggs in the shallows, they become exhausted and die. Now the rivers are full of dying or dead salmon, and the bald eagles simply wade into the shallows and pull them out. Hundreds of bald eagles gather for the annual feast; in mid-November as many as 4,000 birds have been counted fishing along a 10-mile (16-km) stretch of the Chilkat River in Alaska.

Bald eagles also prey on other birds, especially seabirds and wildfowl. They may dive on seabirds from a height, almost like giant peregrines (*Falco peregrinus*), or ambush them as they paddle in the water by flying at low

High Rise

When a bald eagle needs to gain height while scanning the ground for food, it does not waste energy hauling itself aloft with powerful wingbeats. Instead, it finds a thermal (an air current rising from a patch of warm ground) and then circles in the rising air with its broad wings outspread. The rising air carries it up like an elevator; and when the bird is high enough, it can leave the thermal and glide across country until it finds another. It can soar on updrafts from ridges and cliffs in the same way.

The soaring technique is used by many big birds of prey. It is very useful during migration, since the birds can travel huge distances by picking routes punctuated by thermal "hotspots" and updrafts. But they can only travel during the heat of the day and must avoid stretches of open water where there are no rising air currents. That may force them to cross at certain points, like the Straits of Gibraltar between Europe and Africa, where huge numbers of eagles and other migrants can be seen every spring and fall.

level through the troughs between waves. They use similar techniques to catch ducks, geese, and ptarmigan (genus *Lagopus*) on the treeless, hummocky subarctic tundra and may even cooperate to ensure a kill. Bald eagles also take voles, rats, rabbits, turtles, snakes, and even insects.

Paired for Life

At the beginning of the breeding season the mature males and females indulge in spectacular display flights, soaring high over their territory and tumbling out of the sky with their feet locked together. Pairs tend to stay together for life, but they still use display flights each breeding season prior to mating. The main reason pairs stay together is because both birds generally return to the same nest site every season and therefore meet up again with their partner from the previous year.

First the birds check out the nest to make sure it is still usable. Sometimes bald eagle nests become occupied by great horned owls (*Bubo virginianus*); and when this happens, the eagles must start a new nest elsewhere. Some pairs suffer from "nest squatting" quite frequently, so after three or four seasons the bald eagles may have several nests in their territory from which to choose.

Once they have chosen a nest, the birds

⊝ *Bald eagles usually add fresh sticks and other building materials to their nest each year. In time the nest can become an enormous structure weighing up to 2 tons (1.8 tonnes).*

repair it, adding more sticks and soft lining material such as grass or seaweed. When they are satisfied, the female lays her eggs, and both birds take turns incubating them. The eggs are laid at intervals of a few days and hatch at the same intervals. The last chick to hatch is smaller than the others, and competition for food in the nest often means that the youngest chick does not get enough and dies. Therefore, despite the best efforts of both parents, who share in bringing food to the nest, it is quite unusual for more than two chicks to survive to fledging time.

The young birds finally fly at about ten weeks old. At first they are dark all over; but as they grow, they become more mottled with white until they are four or five years old, when they grow their adult plumage and are ready to start families of their own. Most breed for the first time in their fifth year.

Prey Power

Before 1953 bald eagles in Alaska had a price on their heads. The state authorities believed that the eagles destroyed valuable stocks of Pacific salmon, threatening the economy, so they encouraged people to shoot them.

But they were wrong. Predators such as hunting birds very rarely destroy their own food supply. It requires a lot of fish to sustain just one family of bald eagles, so if the fish become scarce, the eagles disappear. That allows the numbers of prey to recover until there is enough to support the predators again. Therefore, the numbers of prey control the numbers of predators, and a big population of bald eagles is a sure sign that there are a lot of fish about.

Hacking Back

If nesting bald eagles lose their first clutch of eggs, the female simply lays some more. Wildlife conservators have made good use of this habit; they carefully remove eggs from bald eagle nests and put them in incubators to hatch. Meanwhile, the eagles incubate a second clutch, and the result is twice the number of chicks.

When they are about eight weeks old, the hand-reared chicks can be reintroduced to areas where bald eagles are scarce, using a technique called "hacking." Each young bald eagle is placed on a man-made nest protected by an enclosure and then fed by humans who stay out of sight. When the eagle is ready to fly, the enclosure is opened so that the bird is able to leave. Since food is still provided at the nest site, the young eagle rarely goes far. By the time it has learned to hunt for itself, it has settled into the area, and with luck the young bald eagle will breed and start a new population.

Back from the Brink

A few decades ago bald eagles were under threat for a variety of reasons. Their taste for valuable fish—particularly salmon—made them very unpopular. In Alaska in 1917 a reward of $2 was offered for every dead bald eagle. However, in 1940 Congress passed the Bald Eagle Protection Act, which made it illegal to kill or harass bald eagles throughout most of the U.S., though Alaska was excluded. The birds were not fully protected by law until 1953, and meanwhile, about 140,000 bald eagles had been shot—more than the entire population of the species alive today.

By the time shooting was outlawed, bald eagles were suffering from something even worse: pesticide poisoning. Like ospreys and many other birds of prey, bald eagles were eating prey contaminated with DDT and similar chemicals. The poisons accumulated in their bodies and had the effect of making their eggs so fragile that they broke in the nest. Eagle populations plummeted, and by the early 1960s there were only some 450 breeding pairs left in the U.S., excluding Alaska.

In 1967 the bald eagle was declared an endangered species south of the 40th parallel, and anyone found guilty of shooting one was liable to prosecution. But the real turning point came in 1972, with the virtual banning of DDT and related pesticides in the U.S. Since then eagle numbers have steadily increased. There are now some 4,500 breeding pairs south of the Canada–U.S. border.

Bald eagles are still suffering from loss of wild habitat and a shortage of natural prey, particularly in the southern part of their range. Many have also died from lead poisoning, caused by eating waterfowl that have swallowed lead shot from shotguns or from fishing lines. Lead shot has now been phased out, thanks to a five-year program instituted by the U.S. Fish and Wildlife Service. So despite these problems, bald eagle numbers are still increasing in most states, and in 1995 the eagle was taken off the endangered list and reclassified as Threatened.

Common name Bateleur

Scientific name *Terathopius ecaudatus*

Family Accipitridae

Order Falconiformes

Size Length: 24 in (61 cm);
wingspan: 74 in (188 cm);
weight: 4–6.5 lb (1.8–2.9 kg)

Key features Long-winged eagle with very short tail;
bare scarlet skin on face and legs; chestnut
back plumage; gray wings with black (male)
or black-and-white (female) flight feathers;
juvenile has blue-green, later orange, bare
skin on face and legs

Habits Usually hunts alone from the air, but larger
numbers may feed together

Nesting Large stick nest in a big tree, often near a
river, built at any time over most of range;
1 egg; incubation 52–59 days; young fledge
after about 100 days; 1 brood

Voice Loud "kow-ah" call

Diet Mainly mammals up to the size of small
antelope, plus ground birds, snakes, lizards,
and carrion

Habitat Open woodland and savanna

Distribution Much of Africa south of the Sahara, as far
south as northern Namibia and South Africa,
but not in dense forests around the equator

Status Range much reduced in south, but common
elsewhere

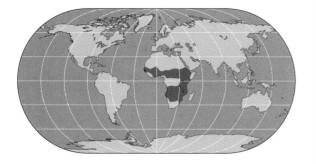

Bateleur

Terathopius ecaudatus

The colorful bateleur is unique among hunting birds: a long-winged eagle with virtually no tail. It is instantly recognizable as it soars over the wooded savannas of the African plains.

SOME BIRDS OF PREY WAIT on a perch until quarry is sighted and then dart down to snatch it up. The bateleur, however, is one of the birds of prey that actively hunts its food. The bird patrols its territory, methodically working its way across the landscape, watching for prey on the ground below. Birds that regularly hunt in such a manner must be able to soar and glide for hours on end with barely a wingbeat in order to save energy. Few do it more effectively than the African bateleur.

Unmistakable Shape

The bateleur's profile is unique. It has immensely long, pointed wings and almost no tail. The body shape is an extreme specialization for soaring and gliding, but is virtually useless for making tight maneuvers in confined spaces. It also makes taking off difficult, so the bird must launch itself into the air with much labored flapping. But once airborne, the bateleur is transformed into a creature of exquisite grace and efficiency, able to soar effortlessly over the broad savannas for most of the day.

Like other soaring birds, the bateleur gains

⊕ Bateleurs often eat carrion, sometimes stealing it from the bills of birds like this whitebacked vulture (Gyps africanus).

SEE ALSO Birds of Prey **15:**8; Vultures and Secretary Bird **20:**8

height by wheeling in circles on rising thermals of warm air, with its wingtip feathers splayed out like fingers to reduce air turbulence. When the bateleur has gained sufficient height, it glides fast and straight across country at an altitude of about 150 feet (46 m), its wingtips now swept back to help maintain speed and steering by tilting from side to side like an aircraft. This tilting or "balancing" action accounts for its name, which is a French term for a tightrope walker. When it reaches another thermal, it starts soaring again, gaining height for the next long glide. It can cover immense distances like this, and bateleurs regularly travel 200 miles (322 km) or more on daily patrols.

As it sails across the savanna, the bateleur watches the ground below for any trace of movement that could betray its next meal. It might be a snake, a ground bird, a grass rat, or an infant gazelle. Once a target is pinpointed, the bateleur corkscrews down in a tight spiral and seizes its victim in powerful talons, usually striking it dead on the spot.

A bateleur can kill prey up to the size of a small antelope, but it is a versatile hunter, prepared to make the most of any opportunity. A swarm of locusts or winged termites may attract several bateleurs, even though they seem ill-suited to eating small insects. In some parts of Africa bateleurs regularly check highways for roadkill. Bateleurs are often casualties themselves, either through road accidents or through eating poisoned bait. Farmers with young livestock view hungry, powerful eagles with great suspicion.

Spectacular Displays

Young bateleurs are nomads, ranging over huge areas; but when they pair up to breed, they claim a territory around a big, shady nesting tree and stay there for many years. Whether they are courting for the first time or pairing up again with a previous year's mate, the start of the breeding season is a cue for spectacular display flights. The birds dive, roll, and pursue each other, rocking from side to side in the air and calling loudly. Sometimes the female flips upside down to present her talons to the male as he swoops past.

If they have nested before, the birds reuse their old nest, refurbishing it with more sticks and a soft lining of green leaves. When the chick hatches, both parents share the task of rearing it. Sometimes a young bateleur reared in a previous season helps, too, by bringing food to the nest. It may be several months before the new arrival is able to hunt for itself and set off on its travels across the African plains.

⊕ *Part of the bateleur's courtship display involves puffing out its chest and pulling its wings back in a statuelike pose.*

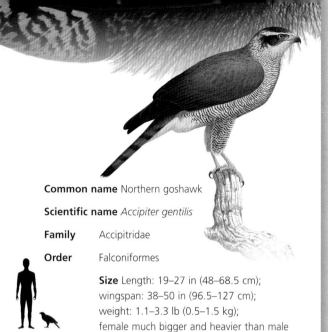

Northern Goshawk

Accipiter gentilis

Common name Northern goshawk

Scientific name *Accipiter gentilis*

Family Accipitridae

Order Falconiformes

Size Length: 19–27 in (48–68.5 cm); wingspan: 38–50 in (96.5–127 cm); weight: 1.1–3.3 lb (0.5–1.5 kg); female much bigger and heavier than male

Key features Big, short-winged forest hawk with medium-long tail; yellow bill base and legs; orange-yellow eye; brown-gray above, pale below with dark bars; very variable over large range; female browner above; juvenile resembles female

Habits Lone woodland hunter, using ambush and pursuit from perch

Nesting Forms longstanding pairs in spring, often reoccupying old nest; usually 3–4 eggs, rarely 5; incubation 35–41 days; young fledge after 35–40 days; 1 brood

Voice Harsh "gek-gek-gek" alarm call, plus mewing "pee-yah" from female

Diet Mainly birds ranging from medium-sized songbirds to grouse and pheasants, plus small mammals

Habitat Typically coniferous or mixed woodlands and forests with clearings

Distribution Forests of northern North America, Europe, Scandinavia, Russia, Siberia, and Japan; in winter North American birds may migrate south as far as northern Mexico

Status Recovering from sharp decline caused by persecution, forest destruction, and pesticide poisoning during 19th to late 20th centuries

The ferocious goshawk is an ambush killer: a fast, agile, yet powerful hunter that specializes in making lightning strikes from dense cover in the cold, dark forests of the north.

THE BIG, POWERFUL GOSHAWK IS THE largest of a group of more than 50 birds of prey specialized for hunting among the trees. Most of these forest hawks belong to the genus *Accipiter*, which includes species like the American sharp-shinned hawk (*A. striatus*) and the Eurasian sparrowhawk (*A. nisus*). They all have relatively short, rounded wings and long tails, giving them rapid acceleration and the ability to maneuver between branches at high speed. Coupled with their keen eyesight and sharp reflexes, the combination is deadly.

⊕ *The goshawk's nest is usually built high in a large forest tree such as a conifer. A nest from the previous year is often repaired and used again. A young bird is shown on the left.*

Forest Hunting Skills

Forests teem with life, especially small birds, and a bird of prey can find all the food it needs within quite a small area. Nevertheless, prey can easily hide among the foliage and undergrowth, and the branches and tree trunks act as a physical barrier preventing a fast, direct aerial attack. But the goshawk manages to overcome these obstacles and turn them to its advantage.

Male goshawks feed mainly on birds such as pigeons and jays, as well as on woodland mammals such as squirrels. The bigger female goshawks can take larger prey such as grouse, pheasants, and hares. They may even catch smaller hawks and owls. Goshawks are opportunists, taking whatever is available seasonally. In spring, for example, they eat a lot of nestling birds, even though they are smaller than their normal prey.

A goshawk usually perches in dense cover, waiting to launch itself into the air and dash after its quarry at high speed. The chase may involve a switchback chase over and under branches, through narrow gaps, and into dense foliage, all performed with amazing

agility. If the target is a grouse or rabbit, the goshawk swoops low over the ground, often almost hovering before the final strike. It may even catch its victim by complete surprise, plucking a bird or squirrel from a branch before carrying it off to a favorite feeding perch.

Goshawks are found as far north as the fringes of the arctic tundra. In winter goshawks that breed near the tundra are sometimes forced to find food further south. Every ten years or so, North American goshawks may fly south as far as Mexico.

Nesting Time

At the end of winter the birds return to their old breeding sites. Mated pairs celebrate their reunion with dramatic aerial displays involving soaring, swooping, and vertical plunges into the nesting woods. Then they repair their old nest or build another. The female guards the young nestlings while the male keeps the family supplied with food, but both can be ferocious in defense of the nest. Most goshawks first breed in their third or fourth year.

Northern Refuge

Goshawks suffered badly from pesticide poisoning in the 1950s and 1960s, and for over a century European goshawks have been persecuted because they take game birds like grouse. Luckily, many goshawks live in remote northern forests where people are scarce, and there at least the bird is doing well.

American Harpy Eagle

Harpia harpyja

Armed with the most powerful talons of any bird of prey, the American harpy eagle can snatch a full-grown howler monkey out of a tree, carry it off, and tear it apart to feed its young.

THE TROPICAL FORESTS OF AMAZONIA in South America are the biggest in the world, and it seems only fitting that they should harbor one of the biggest and most powerful of the world's birds of prey—the American harpy eagle.

The harpy eagle feeds mainly on animals that live in the branches of the forest trees. Attacking its prey without warning, the bird strikes them dead with its huge talons. The talons are thicker and stronger than those of any other hunting bird, and they are matched by immensely powerful legs and feet. They give the massively built eagle the power to deal with some of the most obstinate of all prey animals: those that are adapted for clinging tightly to tree branches high above the forest floor.

⊕ *A harpy eagle usually carries its victim to a perch at the top of a tall tree and then tears off chunks of flesh before swallowing them. Very large prey is dealt with on the forest floor or on the trunk of a fallen tree.*

Common name American harpy eagle

Scientific name *Harpia harpyja*

Family Accipitridae

Order Falconiformes

Size Length: 35–41 in (89–104 cm); wingspan: up to 79 in (200 cm); weight: 8.8–20 lb (4–9 kg); female much bigger and heavier than male

Key Features Massive, relatively short-winged, long-tailed forest eagle; grayish head with ruff and dark crest; gray-black upper parts and breast band, white-barred tail, white belly; white thighs finely barred with black, yellow legs and feet, huge black talons; sexes identical except for size; immature paler

Habits Hunts alone by day over home range

Nesting Stick nest built in crown of very tall forest tree in rainy season; 2–3 eggs; incubation 56 days; young fledge after about 180 days, usually only 1 survives; 1 brood

Voice Loud, wailing "weeeeee"

Diet Mainly climbing mammals such as sloths, tree anteaters, monkeys, and opossums; also snakes, birds, and young deer

Habitat Lowland tropical forests

Distribution Central and South America, from southern borders of Mexico south though the Amazon basin to northern Argentina

Status Threatened by hunters and the destruction of its native forests

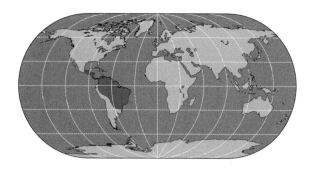

Power Grab

The harpy eagle usually hunts beneath the tree canopy, in clearings, or at the forest edge. It regularly patrols the same range, so it becomes very familiar with the likely places to find prey.

Sometimes the harpy eagle perches in the shade near a river where prey may come to drink, and with its dark plumage the bird can be surprisingly difficult to see in the shadows. As the harpy eagle lies in wait or moves through the forest, it constantly watches and listens for signs of prey. Its hearing is particularly good, possibly because the owl-like ruff of feathers on its head gathers sound signals and channels them to its ears. In the gloom of the forest the eagle seldom gets a clear view, and

the ability to detect faint sounds can be a big advantage.

Sloths are one of the harpy eagle's favorite victims. These peculiar leaf-eating animals creep through the trees in slow motion, supported by stout claws that latch onto the branches like clamps. Their grip is so strong that it may survive even death, and long-dead sloths have been found still clinging to branches high in the trees. Yet the harpy eagle can break that grip by the sheer force of its attack.

When it locates a victim, the bird maneuvers for position and swoops in for the kill, plunging through the foliage and often rolling upside down at the last moment to seize a sloth in its talons. Like goshawks (genus

⊕ *Ruffling its feathers and partly opening its wings to make itself appear even bigger, a harpy eagle adopts an aggressive warning posture. Suitable territories are jealously guarded against rivals.*

⬅ *This well-grown harpy chick has already adopted the attentive stare typical of the species. An item of prey can be seen close by in the nest.*

Accipiter) and other forest hawks, the harpy eagle has relatively short, rounded wings that help it maneuver among the tree trunks and branches, and a long tail for precise steering. Once the eagle has its victim in its grip, it simply carries on flying, relying on its weight and power to rip the animal from its perch. The stresses imposed on the legs are enormous, and one reason why the eagle's legs are so massive is to reduce the risk of fracture.

Sloths typically make up about 30 percent of a harpy eagle's food, but it also grabs tree-living anteaters and porcupines, opossums, monkeys, and parrots. On the ground agoutis (rabbit-sized rodents), young brocket deer (species of deer from Central and South America), and even small domestic pigs form the main prey. Female harpy eagles are able to take much heavier prey; one female was seen to snatch a male red howler monkey estimated to weigh about 15 pounds (7 kg)—the weight of a seven-month-old human baby.

Thanks to its huge talons, a harpy eagle's prey is usually killed immediately. However, if it is still alive, it is dealt a final blow with the bird's heavy, hooked bill before being torn to pieces. The eagle may eat the prey right away, although if it has a family to feed, it selects a big piece of meat—weighing up to 9 pounds (4 kg)—and takes it back to the nest.

Treetop Nesters

Harpy eagles prefer to nest in the crowns of tall, emergent trees (trees growing above other trees in the forest canopy) at heights of 165 to 230 feet (50–70 m) above the ground. Such trees are uncommon even in virgin rain forest; so once a pair find a suitable tree, they stake a claim and return to it when they are ready to breed. The pair build a large nest made from sticks that can be up to 5 feet (1.5 m) across.

As with many eagles, the second (or even third) egg is laid in case the first fails, and it is

Killer Claws

The hugely powerful feet and claws of the harpy eagle are an adaptation for dealing with a particular type of prey—animals that must be ripped from their perches by brute force. The feet of most other birds of prey are equally specialized, although in different ways. An osprey (*Pandion haliaetus*), for example, has fish-catching feet with rough, scaly soles to help grip slimy scales, while a peregrine falcon (*Falco peregrinus*) has bird-catching feet with extra-long toes and talons to penetrate feathers. In contrast, eagles that catch snakes have feet with short, stout toes for swiftly squeezing the life from dangerous prey before it can bite. While the diet of many birds can be deduced by examining their bills, more can be learned about the food of birds of prey by looking at their feet.

rare for more than one chick to survive to fledging age. The female undertakes most of the incubation while the male keeps her supplied with food; but once the chick is well grown, the female leaves the nest to find her own food. Even after it can fly, the young eagle still depends on its parents for 12 months or more, so they cannot breed again the following season. This means that each pair breeds every other year at best, rearing one chick each time.

However, harpy eagles are long-lived birds, so over a lifetime they can still rear plenty of young. Furthermore, pairs are naturally scarce and tend to space themselves out across the forest. If more young eagles were raised each year, they might have difficulty finding enough territories to go around.

Yet again humans are altering the delicate balance of nature. Every year many eagles are shot; and since the eagles breed so slowly, it takes them a long time to replace any birds that are killed. Meanwhile, vast areas of rain forest are being felled for timber and to convert the land into pasture, eliminating the huge old trees that the eagles favor for nesting. If a pair cannot find a suitable nesting tree, they may not breed at all. The harpy eagle population is

Blowout

Many birds of prey, including quite large ones, regularly take whatever food they can find, even small prey like insects and mice. But not the harpy eagle. It is powerful enough to catch and kill big animals, and it usually feeds on them exclusively. As a result, it often finds itself the proud possessor of a carcass that may be several times greater than its average daily food needs.

The eagle eats it anyway, stuffing itself to capacity and then roosting somewhere quiet to digest its outsized meal over the next two or three days. Such a strategy means that the bird may only need to hunt about twice a week and therefore saves energy. Young harpy eagles become accustomed to the regime early, since their parents often keep them waiting several days for a meal. Juvenile eagles have been known to stay hungry for up to ten days, voicing their discomfort with loud, high-pitched screams.

gradually dwindling because of these pressures, and the bird has disappeared from many parts of its natural range. Although not yet in serious decline, it may be only a matter of time before the American harpy eagle's situation becomes critical.

⬇ *Ever alert, a harpy eagle wades into a forest pool to drink.*

Common name Golden eagle

Scientific name *Aquila chrysaetos*

Family	Accipitridae
Order	Falconiformes

Size Length: 30–35 in (76–89 cm); wingspan: 75–89 in (190–226 cm); weight: 6.4–14.8 lb (2.9–6.7 kg); female bigger and heavier than male

Key features Very large with long, broad wings; mainly dark brown with golden-brown crown, nape, and wing coverts; brown eye; black-tipped bill; heavily feathered legs, yellow feet; sexes identical except for size; juvenile darker, with white patches on wings and tail

Habits Hunts on the wing, soaring and gliding, alone or in pairs

Nesting Builds big stick nest on crag or in tree in spring; usually 2 eggs, rarely 1–3; incubation 41–45 days; young fledge after 63–80 days, typically only 1 chick survives; 1 brood

Voice Generally silent, but gives whistling "twee-oo" of alarm and shrill "kya" at nest

Diet Mainly small mammals and game birds, plus carrion, but very variable

Habitat Wild, open terrain—often mountainous—from sea level to summer snow line

Distribution North America, wilder parts of Europe, Scandinavia, northern and Central Asia, North Africa; absent from most of Arctic

Status Recovering from heavy persecution, but still threatened by loss of habitat and food supply

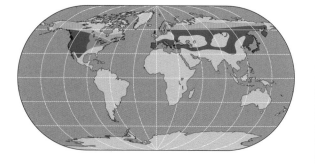

Golden Eagle

Aquila chrysaetos

The majestic golden eagle is an emblem of the wilderness: a spectacular, wide-ranging hunter that finds life almost impossible in regions where the landscape has been tamed by humans.

FEW BIRDS SHARE THE AURA of savage beauty that surrounds the golden eagle. Its great size and killing power make it one of the world's most formidable birds of prey; and when seen in sunlight, its golden crown gives it an impressively regal air. Yet the real source of the golden eagle's reputation may be the rugged landscapes it inhabits. As it soars over the peaks and valleys of some of the wildest terrain in the Northern Hemisphere, the golden eagle is a potent symbol of freedom.

Wide-ranging Hunter

Like most large birds of prey, the golden eagle is relatively rare because each pair requires a large hunting territory. Yet it is found over a huge range that covers most of North America and Eurasia, from the fringes of the arctic tundra to the deserts of Mexico and the Middle East. In sparsely populated regions like northern Scandinavia it often breeds in low-lying country, right down to the coast, while in the Himalayas it may hunt as high as the limit of permanent snow, at 18,000 feet (5,500 m) or more above sea level. In North America the main populations live in the mountain states of Montana, Wyoming, and Colorado, while in Europe golden eagles are most numerous in Scotland and Spain.

In Alaska, northern Canada, northern Russia, and Siberia, where winter temperatures plunge well below freezing for several months, many small animals go to ground and hibernate until spring. Live prey can become scarce, and even carrion can be hard to find in the deep snow. The golden eagles move south to find food, and at such times North American birds may fly as far south as Mexico.

⊙ *Golden eagles have large, powerful bills that enable them to rip into big, thick-skinned carcasses—a feature they share with vultures. Their scavenging habit has given them a bad reputation among farmers, who accuse them of killing healthy livestock.*

In milder regions, like western Europe, the adult eagles generally stay on their breeding grounds throughout the year, but young birds may move south to escape the worst of the winter. At one time the golden eagle probably ranged widely across Europe, but today much of the continent is too densely populated and intensively farmed for its liking.

Aerial Acrobat

Part of the golden eagle's appeal lies in its spectacular flying skills. It spends many hours on the wing every day: soaring high into the sky on updrafts, gliding fast across country, wheeling and sideslipping, and swooping and climbing—all with exquisite grace and elegance. It achieves many of these maneuvers without beating its wings at all, but when necessary it uses deep, slow wingbeats to power itself into the next glide. It can also dive at high speed with half-folded wings like a peregrine (*Falco peregrinus*), either in display or to catch its prey.

A hunting golden eagle ranges over a wide area every day. The actual area depends on the wealth of food available: In Scotland a breeding pair's hunting territory may extend over 15–30 square miles (39–78 sq km), but in the Alps a pair may cover 240 square miles (622 sq km).

Golden eagles take most of their prey on the ground, typically flying quite low and dropping onto their victims in fast, slanting dives. Their main targets are medium-sized mammals such

⊕ Golden eagles hunt over varied terrain with bare crags, moors, forested slopes, and marshes; but generally they prefer areas where the vegetation is low-growing or sparse, giving them a clear view of potential food sources.

Insurance Policy

Golden eagles nearly always lay more than one egg each season, but it is unusual for more than one chick to survive. The first to hatch gets a head start on its younger sibling and bullies it and often steals its food, so it dies in the nest. The elder chick may even kill the smaller one. In some species of eagle this happens so routinely that they never rear more than one chick. It seems a tragic waste. It also appears odd that the parents do not intervene and give the weaker chick its fair share. Yet there is a good reason why they do not.

Unless prey is extremely common, the adult birds can only manage to feed one chick properly. Trying to feed two chicks may overstretch their resources. But instead of laying just one egg, the birds lay a second egg as "insurance" in case the first egg fails to hatch or the chick is weak. Normally the first egg hatches and the chick is healthy, so the second chick is superfluous. But if the first chick is weak, the second will steal its food and survive. Either way the eagles eventually rear a single, well-fed healthy chick, which is a more satisfactory situation than rearing two underfed weaklings that may not survive the winter.

as hares, rabbits, and ground squirrels, plus various game birds. But they are opportunist hunters, ready to snatch young deer or chamoix, fox and badger cubs, rats and moles, even hedgehogs and tortoises—dropping the latter onto rocks to smash their shells. They often pounce on ducks and waders, and are sufficiently agile to catch crows, gulls, pigeons, and large songbirds. Pairs of golden eagles sometimes hunt together to increase their chances of catching elusive prey.

Golden eagles also eat a lot of carrion, especially in winter and early spring, when hard weather and starvation claim the lives of many large animals such as deer and sheep. They sometimes take live lambs, too; but like most

⊖ *The nest, or eyrie, is usually built high in a very large tree such as an ancient pine or on an inaccessible cliff ledge. Golden eagles cannot tolerate disturbance at their nest—one of the main reasons why the birds are restricted to remote regions.*

predators, they usually target weak or diseased ones that would probably die anyway.

Long-term Care

The beginning of the breeding season is marked by breathtaking aerial displays as the birds soar high over their breeding territory, plunge to earth with their wings folded back, and climb again to repeat the performance. Sometimes the pairs grapple in the air, locking talons as one bird flies upside down.

Once the eagles have selected a nest site— they may have three or more within their territory—they set about repairing it, adding stout sticks and green spring foliage. Over the years the nest can grow into a huge pile visible from far away.

The female usually lays two eggs at an interval of three to four days, and she incubates them herself while the male brings prey to the nest. The first egg to be laid always hatches first, and the newly hatched chick usually has an advantage over its nest mate when it comes to sharing food. It often attacks the smaller chick to steal its share, and the youngest nestling often dies of the injuries inflicted on it or simply through starvation.

Fledging does not signal the start of the young birds' independence, however. Although they can fly, juvenile golden eagles are poor hunters. They rely on their parents to keep them supplied with food for several months while they learn how to catch their own prey. Once they become independent, they are still reluctant to leave their parents' territory. Sometimes they are driven south by falling temperatures in the fall. If not, the adults may tolerate them on their breeding territory until the start of the new breeding season in spring. The young eagles do not breed themselves until they are at least four to five years old.

Remote Northern Sanctuaries

Like all large birds of prey, golden eagles have suffered badly from persecution, pollution, and habitat destruction. During the nineteenth century an increase in game bird rearing in

Europe led to an extermination campaign against raptors of all kinds, and big eagles like the golden eagle were at the top of the "wanted" list. Many birds of prey already had prices on their heads, but the introduction of efficient firearms made it possible for hunters to earn a living by destroying them. Many thousands were killed, including most of the golden eagle population. Many also died through eating deliberately poisoned bait, and by the end of the 1800s the species had been virtually wiped out in lowland Europe.

Golden eagles suffered almost as badly in parts of the U.S., such as western Texas. Regarded as a threat to valuable livestock such as lambs, they were regularly killed by farmers. In the 1940s it was discovered that golden eagles could be shot from light aircraft, and the killing became a mass slaughter. For 20 years between 1,000 and 2,000 birds were shot each year in western Texas, until the practice was outlawed in 1962.

The 1960s also saw the golden eagle protected by legislation in many parts of Europe, but by this time it was suffering a new,

Size Differences in Birds of Prey

In most animal species females are either the same size as males or smaller. In birds of prey, however, the females are generally bigger than the males. A female golden eagle can weigh well over 14 pounds (6.4 kg), but a male rarely weighs more than 10 pounds (4.5 kg). The size difference is even more extreme among bird-catching hawks and falcons like the northern goshawk (*Accipiter gentilis*) and the peregrine falcon (*Falco peregrinus*).

Although the reasons for the differences are unclear, the most likely explanation is due to the way the birds care for their young. Females usually incubate the eggs and brood the chicks, while the male fetches food. If prey is scarce, it may be necessary for the female to wait some time for a meal; being bigger gives her the energy reserves to go for longer without food. The smaller male is often more agile, making him a more effective hunter. Therefore the male bird of prey is able to bring more prey to the nest for the female and her young—and also eats less of it himself.

Eagle Eyes

The golden eagle is renowned for its piercingly sharp eyesight—a quality that it shares with other birds of prey such as falcons, buzzards, and vultures. One reason for this is the sheer size of its eyes, which are bigger than human eyes. Each eye also has roughly eight times the number of visual receptor cells per square inch (6.5 sq cm) in its retina, giving far clearer definition of detail. The difference can be likened to the improvement in detail that takes place when a coarse, "pixeled" computer image over the Internet increases in definition as the pixels multiply and get smaller.

Having a high-definition retina is only part of the reason for the eagle's excellent vision, however. A raptor's eye works like a telescope, with a lens that projects a magnified image onto the retina. Because of the magnified image, seen in extrasharp detail, the eagle can detect its prey from immense distances.

⊖ *A young golden eagle eagerly awaits the return of its parent. Competition for food between chicks is fierce, and normally only one of them survives to the fledging stage.*

more insidious threat to its survival—pesticide poisoning. Poisoning was a particular problem in Scotland, where sheep were being routinely doused with sheep dip to kill insect parasites. The dip contained organochlorine insecticides such as dieldrin. When sheep died on the mountains, which is not uncommon in Scotland, golden eagles scavenged their remains and picked up the poison. Dieldrin is so toxic that many eagles were killed outright, and the survivors often failed to breed. The result was the eagles suffered a population crash that was only arrested when the poison was banned in the 1970s.

Today many golden eagles are still killed each year, especially in southern Europe. In the north the birds seem to command more respect, and the populations that survived in the wilder parts of northern Europe and North America are either stable or increasing. Yet they are still threatened by intensive farming, which can virtually eliminate their food supply, and by leisure activities such as hill walking and climbing, which disturb them at the nest. Many are also killed in collisions with power lines. Golden eagles are only really safe in the true wilderness areas of the far north.

Owls

Strigidae, Tytonidae

At nightfall the hawks, kites, eagles, and falcons retreat to their roosts, and small animals emerge to forage for food in the gathering darkness. They are safer in the dark, without question, yet the night has its airborne hunters, too. They drift on silent wings and strike without warning. They are called owls.

Compared with many hunting birds, owls look deceptively benign and even toylike—mainly due to their big eyes, round heads, and thick plumage of soft, downy feathers. But an owl is an efficient killer nevertheless. The fluffy feathers disguise a lean, lightweight body, a sharp beak, and a powerful set of talons as deadly as those of any bird of prey. The big eyes may look appealing, but they are part of a highly adapted sensory system dedicated to the job of locating and targeting live victims by night. Heavily armed and ever alert, owls are among the most deadly of all the world's hunting birds.

Owls live all over the world, from the tundra to the tropics and in every habitat from rain forest to desert. They range in size from mighty eagle owls, which can carry off young deer, to the diminutive elf owl, which preys mainly on insects. A few have taken to hunting by day, and many owls that live in the far north are forced to do so by the 24-hour daylight of the arctic summer. But most owls only come out at night.

⇩ ⇨ *Some examples of owls: spectacled owl (1); elf owl (2); oriental bay owl (3); Malaysian eagle owl (4); spotted wood owl (5).*

Family Strigidae: 22 genera, 160 species, including:

Otus	56 species, including Eurasian scops owl (*O. scops*); eastern screech owl (*O. asio*)
Ninox	19 species, including boobook owl (*N. novaeseelandiae*)
Bubo	18 species, including great horned owl (*B. virginianus*); northern eagle owl (*B. bubo*); Malaysian eagle owl (*B. sumatranus*)
Glaucidium	18 species, including northern pygmy owl (*G. gnoma*); jungle owlet (*G. radiatum*)
Strix	13 species, including tawny owl (*S. aluco*); spotted owl (*S. occidentalis*); spotted wood owl (*S. seloputo*)
Asio	7 species, including long-eared owl (*A. otus*)
Athene	4 species, including little owl (*A. noctua*)
Pulsatrix	3 species, including spectacled owl (*P. perspicillata*)
Scotopelia	3 species, including Pel's fishing owl (*S. peli*)
Micrathene	1 species, elf owl (*M. whitneyi*)
Nyctea	1 species, snowy owl (*N. scandiaca*)
Surnia	1 species, hawk owl (*S. ulula*)
Speotyto	1 species, burrowing owl (*S. cunicularia*)

Family Tytonidae: 2 genera, 14 species

Tyto	12 species, including barn owl (*T. alba*)
Phodilus	2 species, oriental bay owl (*P. badius*); Congo bay owl (*P. prigoginei*)

 SEE ALSO Birds of Prey **15:**8; Owl, Tawny **15:**54; Owl, Pel's Fishing **15:**56; Owl, Snowy **15:**58; Owl, Great Horned **15:**62

Typical Owls

All but 14 of the 174 species of owl belong to the family Strigidae: the typical owls. The most noticeable feature of a typical owl is its big, staring eyes. The eyes are large because they must gather as much light as possible when the owl is hunting. Even the darkest nights are not completely without light, and the owl uses whatever light is available to help it see where it is going. An owl that is kept in complete darkness is very reluctant to fly.

Each eye gathers the light through an extrawide aperture before passing it through a broad lens and focusing it on a curved sheet of sensory cells known as the retina. These cells are mainly of the type called rods, which work well in low light but cannot detect color. The many rods in its retina allow an owl to see in great detail. There is evidence to show that owls can see better by night than humans can by day.

Because of the extrawide aperture, broad lens, and wide retina an owl's eyes would be too big and heavy if they were the usual spherical shape, so they are shaped like flared tubes instead. This means that the eyes cannot swivel in their sockets, so to move them an owl must

5

→ A burrowing owl with its crab prey. Owls are superbly adapted hunters. Huge eyes and acute hearing enable them to fly, and locate prey, in the darkness. Powerful talons and sharp, hooked beaks are then used to deal with their victims.

Deep View

The wide-eyed stare of an owl is particularly striking because both eyes face almost directly forward. This is called binocular vision, and it allows owls to see in three dimensions—a vital ability for a hunter, which must judge distances accurately. Humans have the same ability because our ancestors lived in trees, where judging distances was also vital. If you view your surroundings with one eye closed and then look with both eyes, you can see the difference it makes. Viewed with one eye, your surroundings look flatter; but with both eyes open it is much easier to gauge depth.

Animals that are eaten by predators need to be ever alert to danger. Some have acute senses of hearing and smell. Most prey animals also have eyes placed nearer the sides of their heads to give a virtually all-around view, even though that means they have only a small degree of binocular vision. Woodcocks (genus *Scolopax*), for example, can actually see more behind their heads than in front!

move its whole head. The bird compensates for this by being able to rotate its head through at least 270 degrees, so it can literally look over its own shoulder.

Although a night-flying owl navigates by sight, it hunts mainly by sound. Its ears are hidden behind the distinctive ruff of stiff feathers around its eyes (the visible "ears" of species like eagle owls are just tufts of feathers). The ears of an owl are much bigger than those of other birds, and they are tuned to detect the high-pitched squeaks and rustles of voles and mice in the undergrowth. The ears have huge openings on the sides of the skull and are equipped with flaps. The flaps can move to enable the owl to scan its surroundings, and it is likely that the ruff of feathers helps by directing sound waves into the ear openings.

The owl's extrabroad head means that its ears are spaced widely apart, enabling it to pinpoint the location of sounds in the horizontal plane more efficiently because a sound from one side will be heard fractionally sooner in the ear nearest to it. Many owls also have one ear opening placed higher than the other, and that helps

locate sound sources in the vertical plane (since a sound from a lower source will reach the lower ear opening first). By using the information received from its ears, the owl can fix directly onto its target.

Silent Hunters

Many owls hunt from perches, sitting quietly and listening for potential victims before launching an attack, or by patrolling in a low, slow methodical flight. Whichever method is used, once they are on the wing, owls must keep track of their prey. That means flying silently so they can hear every rustle and take their victims by surprise. Owls are able to do so partly because their wings are very large compared with their body weight. Such an arrangement places less load on the flight feathers, so they do not whistle through the air as the owl beats its wings. A flying owl seems to float through the air, more like a giant moth than a bird.

The flight feathers of most owls also have velvety surfaces and soft fringes that deaden any noise. These "mufflers" probably make the flight feathers slightly less efficient, but that is a price worth paying for a bird that relies on a silent approach to its prey. The few owls that habitually hunt by daylight do not have modified feathers, since they rely on their eyes rather than their ears.

Owls sometimes take insects and even birds in flight, but mostly they catch small animals on the ground. Most species hunt over the same territory all year around, so they know just where they are likely to find prey.

When an owl locates a victim, it usually plunges straight down, guided by its ears and eyes, seizes the prey in its talons, and then swallows it whole. Only the largest victims are torn apart in the manner of birds of prey. The owl digests the meat and then gets rid of fur, bones, claws, and other indigestible parts by coughing them up in compact "pellets."

Territories under Threat

Owls are solitary, stealthy hunters, and many live alone outside the breeding season. Others live in pairs all year, warning other owls off their territory with their hooting calls. Sound is much more useful than visual display at night, so owls are more vocal than birds of prey. Some open-country owls like to share communal roosts, but only the burrowing owl forms true colonies.

The burrowing owl is one of many species under threat. In the U.S. its prairie habitat has been transformed by agriculture, and most of the prairie dog "towns" that it nested in have been destroyed. Elsewhere in the American West the spotted owl is suffering from the destruction of old-growth forests, and throughout the tropics woodland owls are dwindling as their native forests are clear-felled for timber. Some of the bigger owls have been persecuted because they take game birds, and the biggest of all—the magnificent northern eagle owl—has been completely eliminated from much of Europe.

Barn and Bay Owls

Most of the features of typical owls are shared by the barn and bay owls of the family Tytonidae, but the 14 species that make up the family have smaller eyes, distinctive heart-shaped faces, and skeletal differences that include fusion (joining) of the wishbone with the breastbone. The family includes the most widespread of all owls—the barn owl—plus 11 more species of barn owls and the two bay owls of southern Asia and Africa. The barn owl is probably the most intensely studied of all owls, but most of the others are rather mysterious, particularly the African or Congo bay owl, which is still known only from a single individual found in 1951.

⓵ *Disturbed at its roost, a long-eared owl adopts a threatening posture, fanning out its long wings in an attempt to make itself appear larger.*

Common name Tawny owl

Scientific name *Strix aluco*

Family   Strigidae

Order   Strigiformes

Size Length: 14–15 in (35.5–38 cm); wingspan: 37–41 in (94–104 cm); weight: 12–21 oz (340–595 g); female bigger than male

Key features Big-headed; bulky, with broad, rounded wings and short tail; pale or rufous facial disk and dark eye; mottled red-brown to gray above, paler below with dark streaks; very variable; sexes identical; juvenile paler

Habits   Roosts in trees by day; hunts from perch at night among trees

Nesting   Nests in tree hole, rock or wall cavity, or old crow's nest in spring; usually 2–5 eggs, rarely up to 9; incubation 28–30 days; young fledge after 32–37 days; 1 brood

Voice   Sharp "ke-wick"; long, multiple hoot

Diet   Small mammals and small birds, plus frogs, insects, earthworms, and fish

Habitat   Mainly mature woodland and forest; also farmland, parks, large gardens with trees, and even tree-lined city streets

Distribution Europe (except Ireland but including southern Scandinavia), North Africa, parts of western Asia, southern Asia from Nepal to China, and Korea

Status   Generally common and widespread

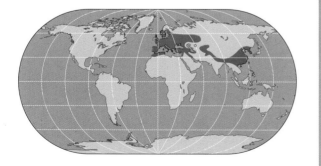

Tawny Owl

Strix aluco

Although few people ever see the tawny owl, its hooting call is a familiar nocturnal sound throughout most of its range—from ancient oak forests to the leafy avenues of great cities.

THERE ARE MANY KINDS OF OWL, but the tawny owl is certainly one of most commonly depicted. Plump, round-faced, with big eyes and beautiful soft, mottled brown plumage, it is like an owl from a storybook. It also behaves in a typically owl-like manner: It flies only by night and proclaims its presence with the classic owl call—a long, quavering ghostly hoot.

The tawny owl is essentially a bird of the forests. It has comparatively short, rounded wings for maneuvering easily through the trees. Despite its apparent bulk, it flies slowly and buoyantly and with barely a sound from its soft-edged flight feathers. It has exceptionally good night vision even for an owl, so it can find its way through the dark forest even on moonless, starless nights that, to a human eye, seem pitch black.

⬆ *Tawny owls often nest in tree holes, particularly ones that were originally made by smaller birds but have enlarged through decay.*

Familiar Territory

A tawny owl occupies the same territory all year around, so it is able to learn every detail of its hunting range. It knows all the best places to find prey; so instead of using precious energy flying back and forth in search of a meal, it usually selects a perch overlooking a likely spot.

The owl then sits and waits, watching for any movement and listening for the slightest noise that might indicate prey on the ground below. It might be a wood mouse searching for seeds or a mole surfacing from its burrow. The owl swivels its head to pinpoint the source of the sound, locks onto its target, glides down, and strikes. The victim is often killed outright by the long, sharp talons; but if not, the owl despatches it with a quick bite to the neck after carrying it back to its perch. Then, with a toss of its head, it swallows the prey whole.

In its natural forest habitat the tawny owl eats mainly voles, mice, and similar small mammals, but it is an adaptable bird that has learned to live in some surprising places. In England some 50 pairs breed in the parks and gardens of London, where they prey mainly on small birds such as sparrows that the owls beat from their night roosts with their wings. They have also been known to snatch fish from ornamental garden ponds!

Tawny owls retire to their own roosts at dawn, perching motionless on branches, in tree holes, or amid dense ivy. Sometimes they are betrayed by small birds that harass them from a safe distance, but usually their superb camouflage makes them very difficult to see. They change their roosts regularly but nearly always stay within their territory.

Night Caller

In spring single males advertise for mates with a penetrating "hooo-hoooo" call. A female may reply with similar hoots, but more often with the sharp "ke-wick" contact call. When the pair come face to face, the male displays on the perch with swaying wing-raising movements and by ruffling his feathers and grunting.

Once formed, tawny owl pairs usually stay together for life. They nest in simple tree holes and cavities, but defend them fiercely against intruders. Tawny owls nesting in town parks have been known to swoop down on people walking too close, often without knowing it, and slash at them with their sharp talons.

The female has the task of incubating the eggs and caring for the chicks, while the male hunts for food. Most young tawny owls breed for the first time in their second year.

The birds are adaptable, and their success at colonizing towns and other unlikely habitats suggests they are less vulnerable to man-made changes than many other owl species.

⊜ *A tawny owl arriving at its nest hole with a mouse. Small mammals form a large part of the bird's prey, but it is a versatile feeder, eating whatever is available.*

Common name Pel's fishing owl

Scientific name *Scotopelia peli*

Family	Strigidae
Order	Strigiformes
Size	Length: 22–25 in (56–63.5 cm); wingspan: 59 in (150 cm); weight: up to 5 lb (2.3 kg)
Key features	Round-headed owl with reduced facial disk; dark eye; gray bill; long legs with no feathering on lower parts; rufous above with fine dark streaks and dark-barred tail; paler below, streaked dark; female usually paler than male; juvenile even paler
Habits	Hunts mainly at night from low perch above water; sometimes wades into shallows
Nesting	In tree cavity, mainly February–April; 1–2 eggs; incubation 32–33 days; young fledge after 68–70 days, usually only one survives; 1 brood
Voice	Loud, penetrating repeated hoot
Diet	Mainly fish, plus frogs, crabs, and mussels
Habitat	Lowland rivers, lakes, and swamps with surrounding forest
Distribution	Forested regions of Africa south of the Sahara Desert
Status	Common over much of central and southern African range, but rare in West and East Africa

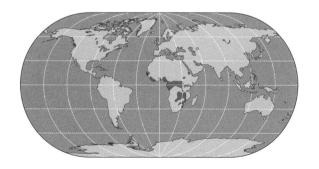

Pel's Fishing Owl

Scotopelia peli

The biggest of the fish-catching owls of Africa, Pel's fishing owl uses its acute night vision to target fish in the tropical darkness, then scoops them from the water with its needle-sharp talons.

BIRDS OF PREY HAVE DEVELOPED many specialized predatory techniques, but most owls use just one. They catch small- to medium-sized animals on the ground at night by flying slowly and detecting their prey with a combination of highly tuned hearing and extrasensitive night vision. It is a very effective method for large birds that hunt in the dark, but it is not the only one. When the diurnal (active by day) birds of prey retreat to their roosts at dusk, they leave a whole range of hunting opportunities vacant, and in some parts of the world those have been exploited by night-flying owls.

Adapted for Fishing

Fishing is a common hunting "niche." By day it is the province of raptors like the osprey (*Pandion haliaetus*), which dives into shallow water to snatch fish it spies swimming near the surface. To catch fish in this manner is quite a feat in daylight, but it is even more difficult at night. Yet the amazing fishing owls manage to accomplish the task.

There are two main species of fishing owl: the four *Ketupa* species of Asia, which are closely related to the eagle owls (genus *Bubo*) and great horned owl (*Bubo virginianus*), and the three *Scotopelia* species of Africa. Pel's fishing owl is the biggest and most widespread of the African birds. It ranges throughout the rain-forest zone of equatorial Africa, as well as further south among the wooded marshlands of the tropics in places like the Okavango Delta of Botswana.

As well as requiring water, Pel's fishing owl also needs big, mature trees to provide nesting

SEE ALSO Osprey **15**:14; Owls **15**:50; Owl, Great Horned **15**:62

sites and plenty of cover and shade from the tropical sun while it is roosting during the day.

A fishing owl's unusual diet is reflected in its appearance. Unlike typical owls, a fishing owl has no feathers on the lower parts of its legs and feet because they would soon become clogged with slime and fish scales. It also has extralong, very sharp talons and rough-soled toes like those of an osprey to give a secure grip on struggling, slippery prey. The naked

lower legs and big, powerful feet give the owl a hawklike look, as does its relatively small facial disk of stiff feathers. In typical owls this disk is very well developed and probably helps them detect and locate faint sounds. But any sounds that fish make are transmitted through the water, not through the air, and they are rarely audible from above. So unlike other owls, which probably depend more on their ears than any other sense while hunting, a fishing owl must rely on its eyes.

Flying down from its tree roost at dusk, Pel's fishing owl selects a perch on a low branch overhanging shallow water where it is likely that fish will swim near the surface. The owl sits and waits, watching for ripples glinting in the moonlight. When it spots a likely target, the bird glides down to seize it in its talons. Often it manages to pluck its prey from the water while barely getting its feet wet, but occasionally it plunges a little deeper. It has also been seen wading into the water from sandbanks in the same way that a heron does.

Most victims are quite small, weighing up to about 9 oz (255 g), but Pel's fishing owl has been known to catch fish weighing 4 pounds (1.8 kg) or more before carrying them back to its perch to eat.

Fishing for the Family

The owls stay on or near their breeding territory throughout the year, the males keeping rivals at bay with loud hoots that can be heard up to 2 miles (3.2 km) away. They nest in tree holes, usually at the beginning of the tropical dry season, when water levels are falling, and the fish are concentrated in smaller areas. That makes them easier for the male to catch when he is feeding the family. Usually only one chick survives long enough to fly from the nest and find a territory of its own. It probably breeds for the first time in its second year.

⊖ *In addition to catching fish like the one shown here, Pel's fishing owl also snatches crabs and frogs, and may even make a meal of a big freshwater mussel, an unlikely prey item for an owl. Note the huge talons.*

Common name Snowy owl

Scientific name *Nyctea scandiaca*

Family Strigidae

Order Strigiformes

Size Length: 21–26 in (53.5–66 cm); wingspan: 56–65 in (142–165 cm); weight: 1.6–6.5 lb (0.7–2.9 kg); female bigger than male

Key features Large and thickset, with massive, heavily feathered feet; golden-yellow eyes; male white with dark spots and bars; female has dark-brown bars; juvenile gray-brown with white face and brown-barred wings and tail

Habits Nomadic; typically hunts from perch at dusk and dawn, but active all hours in daylight of arctic summer; winter activity uncertain

Nesting Nests in shallow scrape on ground, usually on hummock, in northern summer; usually 3–9 eggs, rarely up to 14; incubation 31–33 days; young fledge after 43–50 days; 1 brood

Voice Male has loud, booming territorial hoot; female has hooting, whistling, or mewing notes; alarm call a repeated, cackling "kre-kre-kre-kre"

Diet Lemmings, voles; also rabbits, hares, game birds, wildfowl, occasional fish, and insects

Habitat Mainly open, low tundra; also mountains and moorland, meadows, and saltmarsh

Distribution Found throughout the arctic tundra zones of North America, Scandinavia, and Asia; often moves south in winter or if prey populations crash

Status Scarce but widespread throughout range; numbers probably slightly reduced by some loss of wild habitat

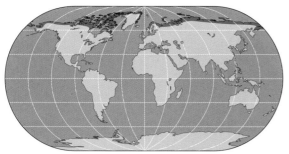

Snowy Owl

Nyctea scandiaca

Adapted for life in one of the most desolate habitats on Earth, the snowy owl finds its prey where it can, often ranging far away from its breeding grounds on the arctic tundra.

BIG, POWERFUL, AND ALMOST PURE white apart from its glaring yellow eyes, an adult male snowy owl is one of the most strikingly beautiful of all hunting birds. It is like a white cat with wings, an impression reinforced by its habit of crouching with its breast on the ground. The female is bigger than the male and, uniquely for an owl, has different plumage. She has dark brown bars and spots contrasting with the white. Both sexes have broad white faces with thick feathering that almost hides their dark, hooked bills. They also have heavily feathered legs and toes, but that cannot conceal their long, wickedly sharp talons.

Life on the Arctic Edge

The dense feathering on the snowy owl's face and legs is insulation against the numbing cold of its home on the tundra—the bleak, treeless, half-frozen land that fringes the polar ice caps. Throughout the long, dark winter the tundra is shrouded in snow, and the ground is frozen solid. But for a few months each year the summer sun defrosts the top few inches of soil and melts the snow to reveal a swampy carpet of plants such as sedges, mosses, and saxifrage.

The whole landscape now bursts into life, with swarms of mosquitoes and other flies attracting vast breeding flocks of waders, wildfowl, and other migrant birds. The plants attract migrant reindeer and caribou in summer, but throughout the year they support small rodents called lemmings that feed beneath the blanketing snow, protected from the freezing wind. The lemmings are the staple prey of Arctic foxes, weasels, ermines, and snowy owls.

In the arctic summer the lemmings are forced to feed in the open, so they make easy targets for predators on the tundra. The snowy owl takes its share, hunting nonstop in the constant daylight to feed its hungry young. But in winter the lemmings are invisible as they forage in their runs under the snow, and they are much harder to find. The snowy owl's acute hearing helps in the task, since it can detect the lemmings' squeaking and scurrying beneath the snow cover. Hunting from a low perch, and homing in with the deadly precision perfected by owls the world over, the snowy owl punches through the snow with its powerful feet and seizes its prey.

Every four years or so lemmings multiply to plague proportions in summer and exhaust their food supply. Then they embark on reckless cross-country journeys in search of new food supplies. Snowy owls and other predators enjoy a feast at such times and raise unusually large numbers of young. But high lemming numbers are usually followed by population crashes, especially in the harsh winter months. By now the birds that breed in the arctic summer have flown south, so the lemming shortages mean that resident predators such as snowy owls have virtually nothing to eat.

Snowy owls are therefore forced to fly off to look for alternative prey. It happens so regularly that snowy owls have become accustomed to a nomadic lifestyle. They roam widely over the tundra searching for food; and if the hunting is particularly poor, they head south to the moorlands and pastures of regions like northern Europe and the U.S. The sudden irruptions (movements of birds in areas outside their usual range) are most frequent in North America because the large area of tundra in Arctic Canada and Alaska is home to many of the world's snowy owls. When lemmings are very hard to find, snowy owls may fly south as far as North Carolina, and strays have even been seen in Bermuda.

Normally these wanderers return north in spring to breed, along with the migrant wildfowl and waders. Even if lemmings are scarce in early summer, they breed so fast that numbers soon build up, and the flocks of breeding birds provide plenty of alternative prey. Snowy owls also take ducks and even medium-sized geese, as well as willow grouse (*Lagopus lagopus*) and snowshoe hares.

⊕ *Thick feathers conceal the snowy owl's big, curved beak—a feature it shares with other owls.*

The heavily feathered legs and feet can be seen clearly in this male snowy owl. The insulation is an adaptation for survival in the cold Arctic.

Ground Nesters

Since there are no trees on the tundra, the owls nest on the ground, although they try to select places that provide a good view over their hunting territories. The male defends the territory with deep hoots that may carry for 7 miles (11 km) or more, and in the perpetual daylight of the arctic summer he performs swooping display flights over the nest site. When he has attracted a female, he courts her with gifts of lemmings to demonstrate his hunting efficiency, since once the female has laid her eggs, she depends on the male to keep her fed while she incubates them. When the eggs hatch, she also needs him to deliver a steady supply of lemmings and other prey to the nest so she can feed the young.

Like the other birds nesting on the tundra, snowy owls must defend their brood against predators such as Arctic foxes. They may try to lure foxes away from the nest with distraction displays—sprawling on the ground

Camouflage

Most owls are superbly camouflaged—for their own protection. Small owls in particular are targets for raptors such as northern goshawks (*Accipiter gentilis*) and may even be killed by bigger relatives such as eagle owls (genus *Bubo*), so camouflage is vital for concealment on their daytime roosts. During the arctic winter the white plumage of a snowy owl performs the same role, concealing the bird from both its enemies and its prey on the snowbound tundra.

However, the tundra is not always snowbound. In milder regions the snow melts in summer, and then the male snowy owl in particular can be highly visible. This coincides with the owls' breeding period, and it is likely that the male uses his conspicuousness to attract females for mating in the same way that the males of many other birds use bright colors. Females, by contrast, have barred dark-brown markings, giving them a grayish appearance that helps them blend in with the rocks around the nest scrape and therefore conceal them from predators.

Female snowy owls, like the one above, have darker plumage than males. The coloration is an adaptation to help the nesting females remain concealed on the ground during the arctic summer when much of the snow temporarily melts.

and flopping around with wings spread, apparently injured and easy to catch. A fox is usually fooled by the hoax and follows the birds as they move away from the defenseless nestlings. At a safe distance from the nest the owls suddenly "recover" and fly off, leaving the fox with nothing.

Variable Numbers

The "boom-and-bust" natural economy of the tundra means that snowy owl numbers have always fluctuated wildly. The owls' nomadic habits also make them seem common one year and scarce the next regardless of the real situation. In fact, it is likely that the owls are losing ground slightly as the tundra is exploited for oil and other resources, but the region is such a vast and inhospitable wilderness—covering some 5 million square miles (13 million sq km)—that the snowy owl will probably always have a future there.

⊛ *A snowy owl adopts a threatening posture, sheltering the chicks beneath its body. Natural predators of snowy owls include Arctic foxes and other birds.*

Family Planning

Owls that live in the cold north often lay more eggs than owls that live in the tropics. The snowy owl may lay up to 14 eggs, while Pel's fishing owl (*Scotopelia peli*) of the African forests rarely lays more than two. Why?

Life is relatively easy in the tropical forests. There are no harsh winters, and local populations of adult owls stay fairly stable throughout the year. Most hunting territories remain occupied, and there are few new territories available to young owls. So if each pair raises just one or two chicks a year, the young birds stand a reasonable chance of inheriting territories and breeding in their turn.

In the Arctic life is very different. Scarce prey in winter may lead to the death of many adult snowy owls, yet in summer the explosive breeding of lemmings and other small animals creates a huge surplus of food. So the surviving adults can often raise large families, and the new chicks make up for the winter losses. The owls vary the number of eggs they lay depending on the prey supply: the more prey, the bigger the clutch. They also lay the eggs at two-day intervals and start incubating the first one right away. This means that the last chicks to hatch are the smallest. So if prey runs short, they get less food than the bigger chicks, die, and leave fewer mouths to feed.

Great Horned Owl

Bubo virginianus

The great horned owl is the night-flying equivalent of an eagle—a formidable hunter that swoops out of the dark to carry off animals as large as jack rabbits.

Common name Great horned owl

Scientific name *Bubo virginianus*

Family Strigidae

Order Strigiformes

Size Length: 17–24 in (43–61 cm); wingspan: 53–56 in (135–142 cm); weight: 1.6–5.5 lb (0.7–2.5 kg); female bigger than male; northern races biggest

Key features Large, powerful owl with big ear tufts; yellow eyes; very variable mottled gray-brown above, dark-barred below; pale or orange-buff facial disk and breast; desert races paler than forest races; sexes similar; juvenile duller, more orange, with shorter ear tufts

Habits Hunts at twilight and night, usually from a perch

Nesting Often uses old nest of crow or hawk, or tree hollow; 2–3 eggs, rarely up to 6; incubation 28–35 days; young fledge after 50–60 days; usually 1 brood

Voice Male gives a series of booming hoots; other calls include screams, growls, and barks

Diet Mainly small mammals and birds, plus carrion

Habitat Anywhere with trees, from extensive forests to wooded farmland and suburban parks, even sparsely wooded semideserts and mountains

Distribution North and South America from Canadian conifer forests south to central Argentina

Status Naturally scarce throughout range, but numbers fairly stable

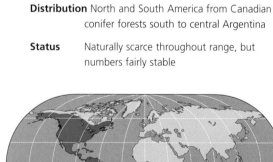

APART FROM THE SNOWY OWL of the arctic tundra, the largest hunters among the owls are the 18 species in the genus *Bubo*: the eagle owls. Found on every continent except Australia, they live up to their name by regularly killing animals far larger than they are able to swallow whole.

The American representative of the group is the great horned owl, which thrives in a huge range of habitats in North, Central, and South America. In the north it lives in the conifer forests that extend to the fringes of the Arctic and may occasionally stray onto the semifrozen tundra. Further south it ranges over the farmlands of the Midwest to the mountain forests of the Rockies and south into the deserts of Arizona, California, and Mexico. In South America it hunts both high in the Andes and down among the mangrove swamps bordering the Caribbean. The bird is extremely adaptable.

The great horned owl can exploit all these habitats because it will take such a wide variety of prey. It favors cottontails and jack rabbits but willingly eats all kinds of creatures, including porcupines, skunks, squirrels, voles, monkeys, crabs, beetles, spiders, and scorpions. Mammals account for about three-quarters of its prey, but it also takes birds up to the size of swans.

Variable Hunting Methods

The bird's hunting technique is tailored to the terrain. On open grassland it flies low over the ground, watching and listening. If there are trees, it hunts from a perch, often near a clearing that gives it room to maneuver. When it detects a victim, it swoops down in a steep dive, leveling out just above the ground to seize it with immensely powerful talons. The owl

⊕ *The female normally lays two eggs but may lay more, especially in the north. Like other owls, the female stays with the eggs and young while the male keeps the whole family supplied with food.*

SEE ALSO Wildfowl **14**:52; Birds of Prey **15**:8; Owls **15**:50; Crow Family, The **18**:90

swallows small prey whole but uses its bill to rip apart bigger victims, like a bird of prey. The owl may eat only part of the carcass, and in the far north individuals often store the surplus in frozen caches and then thaw it when needed by "incubating" it beneath their warm bodies.

A great horned owl needs a lot of food. It makes sure it gets it by driving other owls from its territory and even attacking day-flying hawks and falcons. It frequently catches and eats other species of owl, effectively dealing with two problems at once.

Nest Borrowers

Each pair usually occupies the same territory for many years, but not necessarily the same nest site. They often take over nests built high in the trees by day-flying raptors such as the red-tailed hawk (*Buteo jamaicensis*), but then they allow the hawks to reclaim their property the following season. They may also adopt disused heron nests in active heron colonies.

In years when large prey is easy to find, the male may bring too much to the nest, and it becomes littered with discarded fragments of meat. In lean years the last chicks to hatch usually die; and in northern and prairie regions

⊕ *With its earlike feathers flattened against its head to improve aerodynamics, a great horned owl quarters the ground in the Northwest Territories, Canada.*

where prey numbers regularly rise and fall, the numbers of great horned owls rise and fall, too. Most young first breed when three years old.

Legally Protected

Although the great horned owl is adaptable, it suffered from the destruction of temperate forest in the early years of U.S. colonization, and more recently it was persecuted because it took valuable game birds. Today it is legally protected, but large prey has become so scarce in many areas that the owls must feed on smaller animals such as voles, which affects their breeding success. In the wilder parts of their range, like the taiga forests of the north, great horned owls are still common, however.

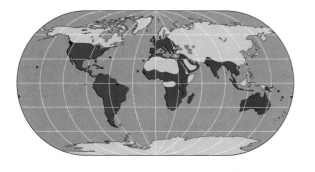

Common name Barn owl

Scientific name *Tyto alba*

Family   Tytonidae

Order   Strigiformes

Size Length: 12–17 in (30.5–43 cm); wingspan: 33–37 in (84–95 cm); weight: 7–25 oz (198–709 g); female larger than male

Key features Medium-sized owl; heart-shaped face; dark eyes; long, densely feathered legs; plumage very variable, typically golden-buff and gray with dark spots above, dark-spotted white to buff below; many races darker above, with orange-buff underparts; juveniles similar

Habits   Normally hunts alone at night, patrolling open ground with low, slow buoyant flight; also hunts from perch; occasionally active by day

Nesting Typically uses hole in tree or cliff, ruin, or farm building, sometimes abandoned bird nest; usually 4–7 eggs, but up to 16; incubation 29–34 days, young fledge after 55–65 days; 1–2 broods, rarely 3

Voice   Shrill, eerie shriek; also snoring, wheezing, hissing, and yapping sounds at nest

Diet   Small mammals such as mice and voles; also small birds, reptiles, frogs, fish, and insects

Habitat Favors farmland, grassland, or marshes; needs hollow trees, rock crevices, barns, or ruined buildings for nesting

Distribution America south of Great Lakes, western Europe, Africa except Sahara Desert, southwest and southern Asia, Southeast Asia, and Australia

Status   Not globally threatened; declining in North America and Europe through pesticide use and loss of grassland habitat and nest sites

Barn Owl

Tyto alba

The spine-chilling shriek of the barn owl pierces the night over fields and pastures throughout much of the world, but it is becoming a rare sound in the intensively farmed landscapes of the West.

FOR MOST PEOPLE A BARN owl is a ghostly white vision caught in the car headlights. For a second or two it seems held in the glare, its black eyes framed by the pristine white of its heart-shaped face. Then it is gone, floating away over the fields and into the night.

A Special Owl

A barn owl has unusual anatomical features that indicate a different ancestry from most other owls. They include a heart-shaped facial disk, relatively small eyes, and curiously serrated middle claws. So zoologists classify it in a different family from the "typical owls," along with 11 more species of barn owl and the two bay owls (genus *Phodilus*) of Asia and Africa.

The eyes of a barn owl give a clue to its nature. Like most other owls, it hunts by night, often when there is very little light. The eyes of typical night-hunting owls are extremely large, enabling them to gather as much light as possible when flying in woodland. But the barn owl's eyes are smaller. Although they are sensitive enough to enable the bird to navigate over its preferred hunting grounds of open grassland, they are probably not so important for hunting, when the bird relies on its ears.

A barn owl has supersensitive ears. They are linked to a specialized array of nerve cells in its brain. Each cell responds to audible signals received from a small part of the bird's environment. The sounds are then mapped on the cell array to create a sonic image, just as light creates a visual image on the retina of the eye. Furthermore, one of the barn owl's ears is set higher on its head than the other, so it can locate sounds in the vertical as well as horizontal dimension. And since the movable

⊖ *A barn owl can locate the rustle of a mouse in absolute darkness, making an attack that is unerringly accurate. It makes the barn owl one of the most efficient night hunters on Earth and probably accounts for the way it has spread over much of the globe.*

⊖ *Barns and other farm buildings are favorite roosting and nesting sites for barn owls. Hay bales make comfortable and secure hiding places.*

Flying Hunter

Owls normally hunt from perches, but the barn owl habitually hunts on the wing. It flies slowly and silently a few feet above ground level, methodically quartering the terrain to check for prey. It may glide, hover, or sideslip, all the while keeping its face pointing down to pick up any telltale squeaks or rustles. When it locates something, it usually hovers and then swoops down in a glide, throwing its long legs forward to seize its victim with outspread talons.

In complete darkness the owl uses a slightly different tactic, plunging headfirst to keep the target directly aligned with its ears and only throwing its head back and swinging its feet forward at the last moment. This maneuver has only been studied using infrared imaging equipment because the owl employs it when it is far too dark for human observers to see.

flaps on its ears allow the owl to direct them toward sound sources, this may enable it to pinpoint distance as well, adding a third dimension. Other owls have similar abilities, but the barn owl seems to rely on them heavily.

A barn owl swallows nearly all its prey whole, even animals as large as rats. A roosting owl will sometimes sit for hours with the tail of a rat hanging from its mouth while the rest is in its stomach being digested. Eventually it ejects

Owl Pellets

Like most owls, the barn owl normally preys on small animals and swallows them whole. In the process it gulps down a lot of material that it cannot digest: fur, feathers, teeth, bones, claws, beaks, and the hard external skeletons of insects such as beetles. The owl's digestive system processes all the different prey items, digesting what is useful and getting rid of the rest. It does so by compressing the waste matter into a compacted lump enclosed in a feltlike mass of fur or feathers known as a pellet and ejecting it through the mouth. Birds of prey also eject pellets, but only to discard indigestible material that they have swallowed by mistake.

Many owls cast up their pellets at random, but some, like the barn owl, habitually produce them at their favored roosting sites. That enables a particular owl's pellets to be collected and taken apart to discover what the owl has been eating. In practice it is not as easy as it might seem because some bones are difficult to identify, and soft-bodied creatures like earthworms—which may be a significant part of an owl's diet—are almost completely digested. But by studying its pellets, zoologists now know more about the diet of the barn owl than that of any other hunting bird.

⊕ A male barn owl brings a mouse to his young brood. As with other owl species, the male hunts for the family while the female guards the eggs and chicks.

the skin and bones as a compact pellet. Barn owls generally use the same sheltered roosts for months or even years, and the pellets can accumulate in deep layers.

The roosts are often in church towers, abandoned buildings, or barns—the latter accounting for the owl's name. Originally the birds used hollow trees and similar cavities near areas of open country that suited their hunting style; but when people started clearing the landscape for farming, they provided more hunting opportunities for barn owls as well as warm, dry roosts in their farm buildings.

Providing accommodation was not entirely accidental. Barns were once used for storing grain, so they attracted vermin such as rats and mice. The barn owl is a very efficient rat catcher, with rats forming up to 60 percent of its diet by weight, so it makes a useful ally for the farmer. In some countries, such as the

Netherlands, farmers traditionally built their barns with special access doors for barn owls, which were only too eager to take up residence. The easy pickings on farms allow the owls to raise large families, so unusually the barn owl has actually benefited from the transformation of its natural habitat into farmland. It is another reason for the barn owl's worldwide success.

As well as rats and mice, barn owls also eat a lot of voles. These small rodents are related to lemmings and, like lemmings, voles periodically undergo population explosion cycles. When vole numbers increase, barn owl numbers also increase because the more voles there are, the more owl chicks each pair can feed. When the local vole population collapses, there are too many barn owls for the food available. Many owls starve, particularly in winter, but others become nomads. Nomadic birds are generally young adults with no territories of their own. They wander far and wide. Although many die of exhaustion, a few manage to claim territories, mate, and have young, spreading the species even further.

Quick Breeders

Barn owls can breed when less than a year old, the male courting the female with a variety of strange postures in the gloom of their chosen nest site. The nest is often in the same old building or hollow tree as the daytime roost used throughout the year, although nests have been recorded in unlikely places—including 33 feet (10 m) down an abandoned well.

The female usually lays about six eggs, but she may lay many more if prey is abundant. The first chicks to hatch get a head start on the others and are generally the first to feed when prey is brought to the nest. If there are plenty of voles, it makes little difference, because the eldest chicks cannot eat it all. But if prey becomes harder to find, the younger chicks go hungry and may starve. The female sometimes feed these casualties to the surviving chicks. It may seem like a callous act, but it can make the difference between raising at least one

chick or none at all. If all the chicks die, the birds often lay another clutch.

Barn owls normally manage to rear most of their chicks, and one pair in South Africa reared 12 chicks from a single nesting attempt. The ability to exploit abundant food has given the barn owl an advantage over some slower-breeding species, and over most of its range the species is flourishing. In North America and Europe it is doing less well, however, and in some areas it has declined steeply.

Declining Populations

One reason for the decline is the very feature that made the owl successful in the first place: its ability to exploit farmland and farm buildings. It served the bird well for 1,000 years or more, but the past 50 years have seen a revolution in agriculture. Machines have taken over from horses, and old-style mixed farming is far less common. Instead of being stored in barns and stacks, grain is swept off the field with combine harvesters and sealed in special rat-proof metal silos. As a result, the rough

Mobbing

Owls are secretive creatures. They mostly hunt by night and spend the day concealed in sheltered roosts. Barn owls in particular often hide from view in the shadowy recesses of old buildings, and most tree-roosting owls choose perches where their camouflage makes them virtually invisible. Despite trying to hide, roosting owls are frequently discovered by small birds. The birds may be part of the owl's regular prey; but instead of escaping while they can, they harass the owl by fluttering around it, calling excitedly. They do the same to perched birds of prey—even bird killers like the peregrine (*Falco peregrinus*)—and may pursue them through the air.

Such activity is known as "mobbing." Mobbing looks risky; but since most hunters rely on surprise, it is not as dangerous as it seems. Yet why do birds do it? Mobbing is most common in areas where the mobbing birds breed, so they may be trying to drive the predators away from their nesting sites. They may also be alerting others to danger or teaching young birds to recognize their enemy. Or they may simply be attempting to drive an intruder out of their territory.

Enemy Alien

Over most of the world barn owls are highly beneficial to humans. They kill vermin, particularly rats. In some areas where rats are a major problem the owls are encouraged to nest in specially provided nestboxes. This proved very successful in Malaysia in the late 1980s, when 200 nestboxes built on a rat-infested plantation attracted some 190 pairs of barn owls.

Yet sometimes the barn owl itself becomes a pest. In the 1950s it was introduced for rat control on the Seychelles, a group of islands in the Indian Ocean that had no native barn owls. The owls found the rats more elusive than the local birds, and within 12 years they had wiped out two populations of terns and were threatening the survival of other rare species such as the Seychelles kestrel (*Falco araea*). Now the barn owl itself is classed as vermin on the Seychelles.

pasture that the owls prefer to hunt over is becoming scarce, the places that they use as roosting and nesting sites are disappearing, and so is part of their food supply.

Rats and mice are also routinely controlled with poisons, but many farm rats have become resistant to standard rat poisons. So farmers now use chemicals that are up to 600 times more lethal. A barn owl can die after eating just a couple of mice poisoned with one of these substances. In the 1990s a chemical rat-control program in northeastern Australia also killed 80 percent of the local barn owl population.

Barn owls also suffered from poisoning by DDT and similar pesticides in the 1950s and 1960s, since these substances were widely used on farmland. When farmers stopped using DDT-type pesticides in North America and Europe in the 1970s, barn owl numbers recovered a little, but the other problems remain. Many barn owls also get killed colliding with cars while flying low across roads at night. After centuries of profitable partnership with humans it appears the barn owl no longer benefits in some places.

⊖ *The four well-grown barn owl chicks seen here still reflect the differences in size caused by the fact that the eggs are laid two or three days apart and hatch in order.*

Swifts

Apodidae, Hemiprocnidae

Most hunting birds are fast and agile on the wing to enable them to outmaneuver and catch their prey. But for sheer mastery of the air no hawk or owl can compete with the swifts. For these mostly small, dark, long-winged birds do not just use the sky as a hunting ground or to get from place to place. They live in it, just as fish live in the ocean. Indeed, the only time many swifts land is when they breed.

Typical Swifts

The great majority of swifts belong to one family: the Apodidae. The name means "lacking legs," since the legs of a typical swift are reduced to tiny appendages. A swift cannot walk or hop like other birds, and if accidentally forced to land on the ground, it is virtually helpless. Its feet have strong claws, but they are strictly for clinging to perches at their nesting sites or night roosts. The most aerial species do not roost at all, but apparently sleep on

the wing. A Eurasian swift may stay aloft for up to three years, only landing to lays its eggs and rear its chicks.

High Life

The air provides everything swifts need. They prey on small flying insects such as flies and beetles, as well as infant spiders that disperse by drifting through the air on silk threads. A swift drinks by swooping down to snatch a mouthful of water from a lake or river. Breeding birds even gather nesting material in flight: Some collect feathers, dried grass, and other windblown debris from the air, while others, like the American chimney swift, snap small twigs off trees as they hurtle past.

Swifts are equipped for their highly aerial way of life with long, narrow, pointed wings. Such a wing shape is called "high aspect," and it is ideal for gliding and soaring. It allows a swift to ride the wind and rising air currents almost effortlessly and may also explain how it can stay aloft when it is asleep. Yet a swift can also fly very fast, outpacing most birds except the northern hobby (*Falco subbuteo*)—a falcon that occasionally catches birds in midair. Such speeds are normally reserved for displays over breeding sites, since catching airborne insects requires agility rather than speed.

Bulk Catch

Typical swifts hunt in the open sky, wheeling and swooping to gather the insects that swarm in the air. A swift has a small bill but a very wide gape, allowing it to scoop its prey from the air like an airborne trawl net. A bird feeding its young may catch over 1,000 insects at a time like this, storing them in its throat and delivering them to the nest in a tightly packed mass.

Such large catches are possible only when insects are flying in large numbers, so swifts that breed in northern regions, such as the Eurasian, alpine, and chimney swifts, are forced to fly south when airborne insects become scarce in late summer. They travel huge distances at high speed—alpine swifts can cover 1,000 miles (1,610 km) in three days—to hunt in the tropical skies of South America, Africa, and Australia before returning north in spring to reoccupy their old nesting sites.

Family Apodidae: 21 genera, 92 species, including:	
Aerodramus	23 species, including Indian swiftlet (*A. unicolor*); Philippine swiftlet (*A. amelis*); Himalayan swiftlet (*A. brevirostris*); Seychelles cave swiftlet (*A. elaphra*); Tahitian swiftlet (*A. leucophaeus*)
Apus	14 species, including Eurasian swift (*A. apus*); African black swift (*A. barbatus*); pallid swift (*A. pallidus*); fork-tailed swift (*A. pacificus*); white-rumped swift (*A. caffer*)
Chaetura	9 species, including chimney swift (*C. pelagica*); lesser Antillean swift (*C. martinica*); Vaux's swift (*C. vauxi*); short-tailed swift (*C. brachyura*)
Cypseloides	7 species, including sooty swift (*C. fumigatus*); white-chinned swift (*C. cryptus*); great swift (*C. major*)
Hirundapus	4 species, including needle-tailed swift (*H. caudacuta*); silver-backed needletail (*H. cochinchinensis*)
Streptoprocne	3 species, including cloud swift (*S. zonaris*)
Cypsiurus	2 species, including African palm-swift (*C. parvus*)
Tachymarptis	2 species, including alpine swift (*T. melba*)

Family Hemiprocnidae: 1 genus, 4 species	
Hemiprocne	including crested tree swift (*H. longipennis*); lesser tree swift (*H. comata*); mustached tree swift (*H. mystacea*)

 SEE ALSO Birds of Prey **15**:8; Owls **15**:50; Swift, Eurasian **15**:72; Swiftlet, Indian **15**:76; Swallow Family, The **15**:94

Nesting Colonies

Swifts are sociable birds. They hunt and display together, and species that roost on perches for the night often cluster in huge numbers. The American chimney swift, for example, is named for its habit of roosting and nesting in tall chimneys: Over 12,000 individuals have been found roosting inside a single flue. A preference for man-made nesting sites is shared by the Eurasian swift, which nearly always nests on buildings or in roof spaces. Other species prefer more inaccessible sites, the most astonishing being the cloud swifts of South America; they nest on the cliffs behind torrential waterfalls and must fly in and out through the falling water. In the Himalayas colonies of swiftlets nest in limestone potholes 230 feet (70 m) below ground, and in Borneo similar swiftlets nest in caves in vast colonies of up to a million birds.

Tree Swifts

Most swifts have weak legs and feet and are poorly equipped for perching, but the three species of tree swift in the tropical Asian family Hemiprocnidae have stronger legs that enable them to settle on treetops. Instead of taking and eating their victims during continuous aerial patrols like other swifts, they hunt from the perch like swallows, darting out to snatch prey from the air and returning to the perch to eat it.

Tree swifts nest in the trees, each pair building a flimsy nest cemented to the side of a small branch with saliva. The nest is just big enough to contain a single egg, which is glued in place for security, but it is too fragile to bear the weight of an incubating bird. So the tree swift perches on the branch with just its breast feathers covering the egg. Soon after it hatches, the nestling must perch on the branch, too, since the nest cannot bear its weight either.

⬆ ➡ *Examples of swifts: African palm-swift (1); alpine swift (2); lesser tree swift (3); mustached tree swift (4); crested tree swift (5).*

Common name Eurasian swift

Scientific name *Apus apus*

Family   Apodidae

Order   Apodiformes

Size Length: 6.5 in (16.5 cm); wingspan: 16.5–19 in (42–48 cm); weight: 1.3–1.8 oz (37–51 g)

Key features Large swift with long, curved, sharply pointed wings; deeply forked tail; black-brown with paler upper surfaces to flight feathers; off-white chin and throat; juvenile darker with larger throat patch

Habits   Strictly aerial except when on nest; hunts by day

Nesting   Normally in small colony in roof space of building, hollow tree, or crevice; usually 2–3 eggs (rarely 1–4); incubation 18–27 days; young fledge after 37–56 days depending on food supply dictated by weather; 1 brood

Voice   Shrill scream in flight; rapid chirruping at nest

Diet   Small flying insects and airborne spiders

Habitat   The air over all types of terrain from forests to semideserts; often over towns and cities

Distribution Europe and Asia, from Ireland east to northern China and from northern Scandinavia south to northern Africa, Iran, and sub-Saharan Africa

Status   Increasing in some parts of Europe, possibly declining in others; not globally threatened

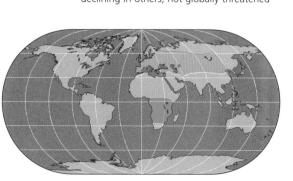

Eurasian Swift

Apus apus

Eating, drinking, mating, and sleeping on the wing, the astonishing Eurasian swift is the most aerial of all birds, capable of spending months or even years in the air without once coming down to land.

MOST OF THE 95 OR SO SWIFT species spend their lives in the warm tropics, where they can be sure of a steady supply of airborne insect prey throughout the year. But a few species fly north to feast on the abundance of insects that hatch during the northern summer. They take advantage of the seasonal wealth of prey to raise their young, then return to the tropics when the insects become scarce.

Of the migrants, none flies farther north than the Eurasian swift, which penetrates as far as the shores of the Arctic Ocean in northern Russia. Many of the birds that reach such regions have flown all the way from South Africa, a distance of 6,000–7,000 miles (9,660–11,265 km). They stay for less than three months before returning to the tropics. It seems hardly worth the trip, but a journey halfway across the world may mean little to a bird that spends most of its life in the air. This is borne out by the fact that some of the migrants are too young to breed. Since they have no extra mouths to feed, the immature birds could almost certainly find enough to eat in the African skies, yet they still accompany the older birds on the arduous trip north.

⤓ *The Eurasian swift may mate on the wing, locked together in a fluttering glide for the few seconds it takes.*

⊙ *A Eurasian swift launches itself into the air from its nesting site high in a crevice on a building in Italy. The hollow nest is built in spring, using feathers and vegetation fragments glued together with saliva.*

Heralds of Spring

The swifts appear in the skies of northern Europe in late April or early May. On fine days the birds circle high in the air, pursuing their insect prey with short bursts of rapid wingbeats punctuated by long stiff-winged glides. On windy, cold, or wet days they hunt lower down or over water, where the insect supply is more plentiful. While hunting they fly quite slowly, since that allows them to loop, dart, and stall to snatch every insect within range. Most of their victims are small bugs, beetles, and flies: A study of more than 11,000 insects taken by Eurasian swifts in Germany found that over half were sap-sucking bugs such as aphids.

When they are not hunting, and especially toward dusk, the swifts swoop around the rooftops in rapid aerial chases, giving high, screaming calls as their underwings flash in the dim light. Many of the birds in the noisy groups are immature individuals. But the excitement is contagious, and mature breeding birds often join in the activity for a while before returning to their nests.

At sundown the screaming parties of non-breeding birds circle, tighten, and start to climb with rapid wingbeats. They rise high in the air to 4,000–6,000 feet (1,220–1,830 m) above ground level and spend the night circling with slow wingbeats interspersed with short glides. In this state they are flying on "autopilot" and are effectively asleep on the wing. They drift on the breeze, while far beneath them the bats take over their insect-hunting niche in the warm summer night.

Faithful Partners

Eurasian swifts always return to the same breeding colonies, and pairs that have bred in previous seasons meet and breed again. They sometimes mate in the air. But more commonly

⬆ *Its food pouch clearly bulging, a parent returns to the nest with food for its chicks.*

they mate at the nesting colony, which is nearly always in a building of some kind, either under the eaves or inside the roof.

The preference for man-made nesting sites is probably one reason why the Eurasian swift is such a successful, widespread species. As humans become ever more numerous, so do their buildings, and the swifts have made the most of the opportunity to exploit sheltered places to rear their young. Some swifts still nest in hollow trees in ancient forests, as they probably have for thousands of years, but that is unusual. For a Eurasian swift the ideal nest

site is a warm, dry undisturbed roof space with access that allows it to fly straight onto its nest.

The birds nest in colonies of up to 40 pairs, exceptionally 100. The nest is just a ring of dried grass, feathers, thistledown, and other airborne flotsam gathered in flight and glued together with the birds' sticky saliva. All swifts use saliva for this purpose and develop vastly enlarged salivary glands during the nest-building period to ensure a good glue supply. The pair take turns incubating the eggs; and when the chicks hatch, they are brooded by one parent while the other goes hunting.

Now the reason why swifts migrate to northern latitudes to breed becomes clear. In early summer the northern skies swarm with small insects, and there are more hours of daylight than in the tropics. Therefore the swifts can keep hunting for far longer than they could in the tropics. In good weather a hunting swift may gather over 1,000 insects in less than 30 minutes, packing them into a tight ball in its throat before taking them back to the nest. There the insect ball is shared among the young, and the adult leaves to gather more insects to make another ball.

After about 14 days each chick is big enough to swallow a complete food ball whole, and by this time both parent birds are hunting. In nice weather insects are abundant, and the young swifts may be ready to leave the nest within five weeks. If the weather is poor, there are fewer flying insects to be caught, and the chicks develop more slowly.

Time to Leave

By the end of July most of the adult flying insects have bred, and they are starting to die off. Now the newly fledged young swifts prepare to make the long trip to Africa—a journey they seem to achieve entirely by instinct, since they leave before the adults. But within a week or two they are all winging their way south across southern Europe and southwest Asia, around the Mediterranean, and across the deserts to the grasslands of the African tropics.

Lousy Parasites

Eurasian swifts are plagued by blood-sucking parasites called louse-flies. These heavily armored, virtually wingless insects lurk in the birds' nesting colonies and attack both the adult birds and their young. The insects have a talent for avoiding probing bills, and the swifts seem almost incapable of getting rid of them.

Every five days or so each louse-fly helps itself to a meal of blood, extracting a few drops at a time. That may not seem much, but it is a serious loss to a small bird like a swift. Furthermore, each swift may be host to two or three of these bloodsuckers, and there are reports of swifts being found with 20 or more of the parasites clinging to their emaciated bodies.

When they arrive, it is likely that they spend all their time on the wing, riding the air at night just as they do in Europe. Since many of the newly fledged birds spend the next two or three years in Africa before heading north to breed, it means they could fly continuously all that time. Being long-lived birds, they may keep flying for over a decade. It has been estimated that an 18-year-old swift found in 1964 may have covered 4 million air miles in its lifetime—the equivalent of eight return trips to the Moon.

Hard Times

When food becomes scarce in July, Eurasian swifts leave for Africa. However, if airborne insect prey is scarce in the middle of the breeding season—for instance, during a cold, wet spell when insects stop flying—the adult swifts must simply wait until the weather improves. Then insect numbers increase again, and the chicks can continue to be fed.

During lean times an adult swift deals with the problem by retreating to its nesting colony to roost in a torpid (sluggish) state, almost like a hibernating bat. In this condition the bird's body temperature falls, and it uses a lot less energy. It can live off its fat reserves and does not need to eat.

Meanwhile, its nestlings have the amazing capacity to survive for up to 10 days without food. Like their parents, they sink into a semicoma, becoming so cold and inert that they seem dead, and they may lose up to half their body weight. Yet when the weather improves and the adults are able to hunt again, the nestlings revive and continue their development.

→ *The tiny feet and claws of the Eurasian swift allow it to cling to surfaces when it is not flying, but they are useless for walking around on the ground.*

Indian Swiftlet

Aerodramus unicolor

Able to hunt by night and find their way through dark nesting caves using sonar, the Indian swiftlet and its near relatives occupy a niche normally occupied only by the bats.

Common name Indian swiftlet (Indian edible nest swiftlet)

Scientific name *Aerodramus unicolor* (*Collocalia unicolor*)

Family   Apodidae

Order   Apodiformes

Size Length: 5 in (12 cm); wingspan: 12 in (30 cm); weight: 0.3–0.5 oz (8.5–14 g)

Key features Medium-sized swiftlet with shallow-forked tail; dark brown above; pale brown below

Habits Aerial, but roosts in caves; hunts by day and by night

Nesting In dense colonies in caves and artificial tunnels; shallow, bracketlike nest of firm, pale hardened saliva, mixed with varying quantities of plant material and feathers; 2 eggs; incubation and fledging times not known; 2 broods in Sri Lanka

Voice Grating, clicking echolocation call

Diet Small flying insects

Habitat Areas of grassland, scrub, or dry forest with suitable nesting caves from sea level (including small islands) to mountains

Distribution Resident in southwest India and Sri Lanka

Status Generally common throughout range; abundant in Sri Lanka but with local declines caused by illegal nest collection for the edible-nest trade

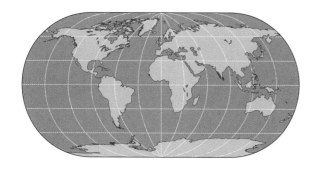

COMPARED WITH BIGGER, MORE SPECTACULAR relatives like the Eurasian swift (*Apus apus*), the swiftlets of the Far East may look rather drab and dull. Yet their appearance is misleading, because they are among the most intriguing of all hunting birds.

There are 28 species altogether. Most of them belong to a group that is often given the generic name *Aerodramus*: the tropical cave-nesting swiftlets of southern and southeast Asia, New Guinea, northern Australia, and Oceania. The Indian swiftlet is one of the best-known. Many of the others are restricted to oceanic islands or remote mountain ranges, where their habits remain a mystery.

Aerial Hunter

Like other swifts, the Indian swiftlet hunts in the open sky, wheeling and diving to scoop up flying insects in its gaping bill. It is quite selective, often favoring particular species of insect, although it may simply be attracted to large flying swarms where it can catch a lot of prey in a short time. The Indian swiftlet hunts by sight, but it is nevertheless often active after sunset, particularly when it has nestlings to feed. Indian swiftlets have been seen swooping through pools of light around street lamps to snatch insects attracted by the light.

The bird can fly confidently at night because it can navigate by echolocation, like a bat. It emits a rapid stream of metallic-sounding clicking calls that resemble the sound made by running a finger along the teeth of a comb. The clicks are reflected by obstacles, and the swiftlet's instant, instinctive analysis of the

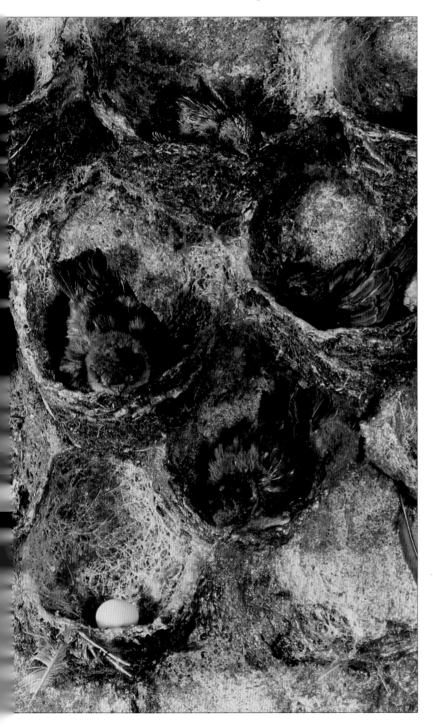

The nests of Indian swiftlets are composed of plant fragments and feathers glued together with large quantities of the birds' saliva. The nests are built in tightly packed colonies in dark caves.

echoes provides it with a sonar image of its surroundings. All swiftlets of the genus *Aerodramus* can navigate by the same method.

Although the bird's echolocation system is efficient, it is far less precise than a bat's. It cannot pinpoint small objects, so the swiftlet cannot use it to locate flying insects. It seems to have evolved as a navigation system for use in the total darkness of the caves that the swiftlet uses for breeding.

Cave Nester

The Indian swiftlet uses all kinds of caves, from coastal caverns to railway tunnels. A big, secluded cave with good access may attract thousands of pairs, which build their nests in tight clusters up near the cave ceiling. The sites are usually some distance from the entrance in permanent darkness, so a swiftlet needs all its echolocation skills to find its way through the cave, avoid the streaming two-way traffic of other swiftlets, and locate its nest among thousands of others.

Indian swiftlets build their nests of debris glued together with sticky saliva, which sets as a firm, whitish solid mass. If suitable nesting material is scarce, some pairs may build their nests entirely of saliva—just like the edible-nest swiftlet (*Aerodramus fuciphagus*) that unwittingly supplies the raw material for bird's nest soup.

Expensive Soup

Edible nests are in such demand that they sell for huge sums. In Hong Kong, the center of the industry, about 2.2 pounds (1 kg) of high-grade nests can fetch as much as $36,000! Since there are roughly 50 nests to the pound, each nest is worth about $330. So it is hardly surprising that the breeding caves of edible-nest swiftlets are regularly ransacked—both legally and illegally—to supply the trade. Each year some 16 million nests are harvested in Indonesia alone, putting tremendous pressure on the edible-nest swiftlet populations.

The demand is so great that other species like the Indian swiftlet are targeted, too, despite the fact that their nests are typically less pure and have a lower market value. In Sri Lanka several local populations have been badly affected, even though the swiftlet is a protected species, and nest collection attracts heavy fines. Luckily the Indian swiftlet is still common, so the species as a whole is in no immediate danger from nest collectors. But some of the other cave swiftlets are declining alarmingly, and it is possible that the huge demand for the nests could eventually drive them to extinction.

Nightjars and Frogmouths

Caprimulgidae, Podargidae, Nyctibiidae, Aegothelidae, Steatornithidae

When the insect-hunting swifts abandon the chase at dusk, their place in the darkening sky is taken by bats. But in some places bats have competition from a group of strange birds that look and behave rather like night-flying swifts or small owls. They are the nightjars, frogmouths, and their relatives in the order Caprimulgiformes.

Most of these birds feed on insect prey, so they live mainly in the tropics and subtropics where their insect supply is guaranteed throughout the year. But several of the nightjars migrate to the temperate regions of North America and Eurasia to breed in the northern summer before returning to the tropics, like migrant swifts. These northern breeders include the American common nighthawk, the whippoorwill, and the European nightjar. Another North American species, the common poorwill, is the only bird known to survive the winter by allowing its body temperature to fall and slipping into a state resembling hibernation in the way that bats overwinter in temperate climates.

Nightjars

The nightjars of the family Caprimulgidae are mainly aerial night hunters with excellent flying skills. They swoop after moths, beetles, mosquitoes, and other insects that fly after sundown. They include such oddly named species as the whippoorwill, common poorwill, and chuck-will's-widow, which are all named for their strange, repetitive whistling calls. The European nightjar produces an even more peculiar call: a mechanical "jarring" or churring sound that resembles that of a small, distant motorcycle. Nightjars are also known as goatsuckers because they were once believed to steal milk from goats, and it is the literal meaning of their scientific name, *Caprimulgus*.

Since these birds must navigate and locate their prey in the dark, they have big eyes in order to admit as much of the dim light as possible. Many species may also be able to detect obstacles by a crude form of echolocation, rather like that used by bats. The birds call repeatedly as they fly, and research on the common nighthawk has shown that it cannot fly at night if its hearing is temporarily impaired. This suggests that the bird listens for echoes reflected from nearby objects and uses them to navigate in the darkness.

Bats can target flying insects using echolocation, but it is unlikely that nightjars can do so. They probably rely

Family Caprimulgidae: 15 genera, 89 species, including:

Caprimulgus	49 species, including chuck-will's-widow (*C. carolinensis*); whippoorwill (*C. vociferus*); European nightjar (*C. europaeus*)
Eurostopodus	7 species, including satanic nightjar (*E. diabolicus*)
Chordeiles	5 species, including common nighthawk (*C. minor*)
Macrodipteryx	2 species, including standard-winged nightjar (*M. longipennis*)
Phalaenoptilus	1 species, common poorwill (*P. nuttallii*)
Podager	1 species, Nacuda nighthawk (*P. nacuda*)

Family Podargidae: 2 genera, 13 species

Batrachostomus	10 species, including Bornean frogmouth (*B. cornutus*)
Podargus	3 species, including tawny frogmouth (*P. strigoides*)

Family Nyctibiidae: 1 genus, 5 species

Nyctibius	including common potoo (*N. griseus*); giant potoo (*N. grandis*)

Family Aegothelidae: 1 genus, 8 species

Aegotheles	including Archbold's owlet-nightjar (*A. archboldi*); Australian owlet-nightjar (*A. cristatus*)

Family Steatornithidae: 1 species

Steatornis	oilbird (*S. caripensis*)

 SEE ALSO Owls **15**:50; Swifts **15**:70; Whippoorwill **15**:82; Nightjar, Standard-winged **15**:84

on sight and sound—nightjars are most active at twilight when they can see their flying prey silhouetted against the sky. A hunting nightjar is helped by its large mouth, which can gape wide open rather like the mouth of a snake. That enables it to engulf several small insects at

⊕ *A Nacuda nighthawk from Brazil flies close to the surface of a lake. The huge gape of its open mouth enables the bird to gather up flying insects with ease.*

a time or even a giant moth with a 4-inch (10-cm) wingspan. The corners of its mouth are fringed with stiff sensory bristles to funnel prey into the gaping trap.

Frogmouths

Although they look very like nightjars, the frogmouths of the family Podargidae have a rather different hunting style. They are relatively poor flyers and usually hunt from perches, targeting insects and larger animals on the

ground and gliding down to seize them. Their sharply hooked bills are much larger than those of nightjars; and as their name implies, they can gape their mouths improbably wide to gulp down victims as large as mice.

Frogmouths live mainly in the tropical rain forests of Southeast Asia, Indonesia, and Australia, where they nest and roost in trees. Like nightjars, they roost in the open in broad daylight and often in clear view. They are hidden from their enemies by their astonishingly effective camouflage, which mimics the bark of trees so perfectly that a roosting frogmouth is virtually invisible even at close range. Ground-roosting nightjars have similarly cryptic plumage that matches the forest floor leaf litter.

Full View

Like others of its family, the standard-winged nightjar spends the day roosting on the ground or on a branch often in full view of potential enemies. It survives because it is disguised by its amazingly effective camouflage. Few other birds can rival the nightjars and frogmouths in this respect. Their mottled browns and grays, flecked with black and white, are a perfect match for tree bark or dead leaves. The birds also have a highly developed instinct for "freezing" at the least hint of danger, often in curious attitudes that mimic broken branches or tree stumps. A threatened nightjar will also flatten itself against the ground to eliminate its shadow and hide the telltale glint of its large eyes by closing them to slits.

Yet sometimes this instinct is their undoing. Nightjars and their nests are occasionally trampled by large animals and people who do not know they are there, and immobility is no defense against fast-moving vehicles. The birds like to hunt over open ground at night and may rest on roads and tracks between sorties. Dazzled by the headlights, they hunker down to protect themselves but end up flattened beneath the wheels.

⊕ *Representative species from the order Caprimulgiformes: oilbird (1); common potoo (2); Australian owlet-nightjar (3).*

Potoos

Like the nightjars, the potoos of the family Nyctibiidae owe their common name to the distinctive call of one species: the giant potoo of the American tropics. Always given at night, the "baw-woo" call is extremely loud and frequently mistaken for the yowling of a cat.

All five species of potoos live in Central and South America. They hunt night-flying insects such as moths and beetles, darting up from perches like nocturnal flycatchers. Like nightjars and frogmouths, they can open their mouths extremely wide, thanks partly to an unusually mobile upper mandible, and that allows them to engulf surprisingly large prey. They also have the exquisite camouflage typical of their relatives, which allows them to roost in the open on branches without being spotted by other hunters such as birds of prey.

Owlet-nightjars

Closely related to the frogmouths, the owlet-nightjars of the family Aegothelidae are restricted to Australia and New Guinea. They are sometimes known as "moth owls," which aptly describes their soft, large-eyed character and mothlike flight. They hunt at night, usually taking flying insects from a perch but also using their relatively strong, powerful legs to pursue prey on the ground. In New Guinea they hunt among the trees, but in Australia— where they live as far south as Tasmania—they often forage over more open country. Like their relatives, they are well camouflaged, but typically roost in tree holes or other cavities rather than in the open.

Oilbird

The one remaining family in the order, the Steatornithidae, consists of a single species: the oilbird. It is not a hunting bird at all, since it feeds entirely on the oily fruits of palms, incense trees, and laurels; but it is remarkable for the

way it always feeds at night and roosts in caves. It finds its way in the pitch darkness below ground using echolocation, like a cave-swiftlet, judging the proximity of the cave walls by producing staccato clicking calls that echo off the rock.

⊕ *The stunningly effective camouflage of the tawny frogmouth is demonstrated clearly below. The two individuals, roosting by day, are scarcely visible among the dead branches.*

Common name Whippoorwill

Scientific name *Caprimulgus vociferus*

Family   Caprimulgidae

Order   Caprimulgiformes

Size Length: 8.5–10.5 in (21.5–27 cm); wingspan: 18–19.5 in (46–49.5 cm); weight: 1.5–2.5 oz (43–71 g)

Key features Medium-sized nightjar with short legs; small bill; big, dark eyes; cryptic plumage grayish brown above; buff cheeks; underparts brown, spotted and barred pale gray-and-buff; male has pale-gray breast band and broad white tips to outer tail feathers; female has narrow buff tips; immature similar but with more buff

Habits   Aerial insect hunter; active at night and twilight

Nesting   On ground in clearing, in leaf litter, often beneath undergrowth; 1–2 eggs; incubation 19–21 days; young fledge after 15 days; often 2 broods

Voice   Male gives repeated, whistling "whip, poor-will"; also short, sharp "quit" and variety of coos, chuckles, and hisses

Diet   Mainly flying insects

Habitat   Forest, woodland, suburban gardens, scrub

Distribution Central and southeastern Canada, central, eastern, and southwestern U.S., Mexico, and Central America south to Nicaragua

Status   Common over much of range, but declining in eastern U.S. owing to loss of wild habitat, pesticide pollution, roadkill, and predation by domestic cats

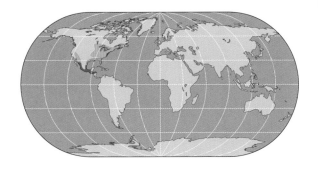

Whippoorwill

Caprimulgus vociferus

Although well known for the way it repeats its name over and over again during the warm summer nights, the whippoorwill is an elusive hunter, usually seen as a flitting shadow as it pursues its insect prey through the dusk.

SUPERBLY CAMOUFLAGED TO THE POINT of virtual invisibility by day, yet relentlessly noisy by night, the whippoorwill can be a frustrating target for a birdwatcher. Like all nightjars, it spends most of the day asleep, either on the ground or perched with its body lying along a low branch, its cryptic plumage allowing it to sit in full view without being noticed. At dusk it stirs itself to hunt and often to call with apparently endless repetitions of the same three notes: "whip, poor-will…whip, poor-will…whip, poor-will…"

The whippoorwill winters in Central America, flying north in spring to the woods and forests of North America. Most nightjars choose more open habitats, but the whippoorwill is always found among the trees. It lives in all types of forest, although it favors oak or mixed oak and pine.

Insect Hunter

In typical nightjar fashion the whippoorwill preys mainly on flying insects, especially moths, pursuing them with great agility on near-silent wings and scooping them up in its gaping mouth. It often hunts from a perch at the edge of a forest clearing, launching itself in short sallies to intercept passing insects, flying low over the ground, and often returning to the same perch. Sometimes it may stay on the wing for quite a while, hawking back and forth over the same patch of ground. Occasionally, it pounces on beetles or worms on the ground.

Repeated Caller

As soon as males arrive in the north in spring, they start singing to claim breeding territories

↑ *Large eyes enable the whippoorwill to see in low light conditions. Long bristles around the mouth help trap insect prey.*

and attract females. A male whippoorwill may repeat his three-note call 100 times in succession and sometimes more; the record is 1,088 calls in a row, so the bird certainly earns its scientific name *vociferus*. The tone of the call varies from region to region: Eastern birds have a clear, warbling note, while southwestern whippoorwills sound more guttural.

Pairs nest on the ground among fallen leaves, often in the shelter of a rock or fallen tree. They display to each other by strutting with fanned tails, the male purring seductively to his mate while she responds with soft chuckling notes. Egg laying seems to be timed so that the eggs hatch toward full moon, allowing two weeks of easy hunting throughout much of the night to keep the chicks supplied with food. By then the young are almost ready

to fly, but it is another two weeks before they are ready to take off on their own.

Forest Recolonizers

For thousands of years the whippoorwill inhabited the vast, mixed forest extending from the prairies to the Atlantic and from the subtropical swamps of the Gulf coast to the southern fringes of Canada. Most of the forest was swept away during the eighteenth and nineteenth centuries; but when the colonists discovered the fertile lands to the west of the Ohio River, they abandoned much of the farmland on the stony Appalachian Mountains, allowing the forest to grow again. This means that in the eastern states at least, the whippoorwill can still find plenty of woodland where it can hunt and breed.

Standard-winged Nightjar

Macrodipteryx longipennis

Common name Standard-winged nightjar

Scientific name *Macrodipteryx longipennis*

Family Caprimulgidae

Order Caprimulgiformes

Size Length: 10.5 in (27 cm), excluding extended wing feathers of male; wingspan: 17–18.5 in (43–47 cm); weight: 1.1–2.3 oz (31–65 g)

Key features Large nightjar; small bill; big, dark brown eyes; plumage cryptic brown above, streaked and speckled grayish-white, buff, and dark brown; underparts brown, speckled pale gray-and-buff; tawny-buff collar; male has white throat patch and elongated second inner primary feather on each wing, discarded after breeding; female paler; immatures resemble adult female

Habits Hunts by night on the wing over open country and clearings

Nesting Male may mate with several females; 1–2 eggs laid on ground; incubation and fledging times not known; 1 brood

Voice Male gives rapid, twittering insectlike "ts-ts-ts-ts-ts"

Diet Flying insects, including locusts, moths, beetles, flies, and winged termites

Habitat Lightly wooded savanna, scrub, forest clearings, and open sandy areas

Distribution Africa south of Sahara Desert and north of the equator

Status Common throughout most of range

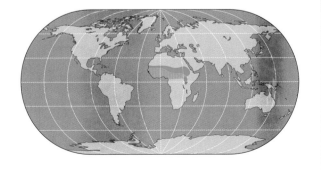

The spectacular, elongated wing feathers of the male standard-winged nightjar are so successful at attracting females that a male may mate with several each season, leaving them with the job of rearing their young alone.

STANDARD-WINGED NIGHTJARS PREY ON FLYING insects such as moths, cicadas, flies, and winged ants, sometimes gathering to exploit swarms of winged termites or insects escaping from bush fires. The birds typically hunt by twilight and moonlight, flying with buoyant agility and snatching their victims out of the sky.

By daybreak the nightjars are back at the roost, usually crouching on the ground among dead leaves and other vegetation and virtually invisible thanks to their cryptic plumage. Even a breeding male is hard to see, because although his plumage is bizarre, it has no bright colors. At rest he sits with wings folded, but with the "standards" outstretched on either side, up to 40 inches (100 cm) apart.

During the day a roosting standard-winged nightjar often sits in the full glare of the tropical sun, yet it manages to avoid overheating by gaping its large mouth wide open and vibrating its throat to circulate air over the exposed mouth lining, just like a panting dog.

Spectacular Wing Feathers

The males of some bird species (for example, peacocks) have extravagant adornments, such as brightly colored plumage or long ornamental plumes, to attract females at mating time. Showy adornments are unusual among hunting birds, however, probably because they make hunting more difficult. Birds of prey, for example, need to be fast and agile, and cannot afford impractical plumage that might reduce their hunting efficiency. But insect hunting is less demanding, and it has enabled the males of

SEE ALSO Peafowl, Indian **11:**52; Birds of Prey **15:**8; Nightjars and Frogmouths **15:**78; Whippoorwill **15:**82

a few nightjar species to develop spectacular plumage whose only function is to attract a mate. The best example of such mating plumage is seen in the standard-winged nightjar. In the breeding season the male sports a pair of greatly elongated flight feathers called standards. Circling a female on quivering, arched wings, he raises the standards so they flutter high over his back, like flags on the ends of two long, flexible aerials. Meanwhile, the male's vibrating wing feathers produce a mechanical "frrp" sound to draw attention to the spectacle.

Males do not perform their mating flights alone. They gather over open ground and display to an audience of females. The group display, called a "lek," gives the females the opportunity to choose the males that produce the finest performances. The most accomplished males may then mate with several females. Once all the available females have mated, they find nesting sites and lay their eggs. The females incubate the eggs and rear the chicks alone. They nest on the ground, relying on their camouflage to protect them during the day; but many lose their broods to prowling snakes, monitor lizards, mongooses, and other predators. If a nesting female is threatened, she tries to draw the killer away with a "distraction display," feigning injury and fluttering away from the nest; she may also hiss and gape wide open her huge mouth.

Flying North

After the males have mated, they fly north to spend the wet season in the Sahel region on the southern fringes of the Sahara Desert, where the seasonal rains normally encourage abundant vegetation and insect life. The females and their young probably follow later, after the young have fledged. The birds return to the southern savannas a few months later to breed, but the precise movements of this species are still not fully understood.

⊕ *The male's long breeding feathers consist of a broad vane on the end of a slender, bare shaft up to 20 inches (50 cm) long—twice the bird's body length. The vanes are dull brown because bright colors are not necessary in birds that fly by moonlight or twilight. They are intended to show up in silhouette against the pale glow of the sky and create a dramatic effect when the male performs his slow, undulating display flight.*

Rollers

Coraciidae, Brachypteraciidae, Leptosomatidae

Hunting birds typically have discreet, even drab plumage, but the rollers are a dazzling exception. Resplendent in glorious shades of iridescent blue, purple, lilac, green, and rich chestnut, they are among the most eye-catching of all birds. Furthermore, both sexes of some species (like the racket-tailed roller) have long tail streamers that may help them distinguish their own kind from other, equally colorful species.

Ebbing and Flowing

Rollers are birds of grassland, scrub, and open forests. They prefer open country; but since typical rollers usually nest in tree holes that are often originally excavated by woodpeckers, they live only in areas where suitable trees are available.

Rollers have a mainly tropical distribution. In regions such as equatorial Africa, where insects are available all year round, species like the blue-throated roller may spend their whole lives in one area. Elsewhere the food supply is usually more seasonal, especially in dry grasslands and semideserts, so the birds migrate back and forth with the ebb and flow of insect life. Many species are partial migrants: Some local populations live in one place, while others come and go. The lilac-breasted rollers of southern Africa, for example, usually stay in one location, while species living in eastern Africa usually migrate back and forth between Somalia and Kenya.

Two species travel much farther. Both the European roller and eastern broad-billed roller breed in temperate Eurasia, returning to the tropics during the northern winter. The eastern species also breeds in Australia, migrating north to the tropics for the southern winter. The birds may fly huge distances, and the European roller is famous for mass movements involving vast flocks of the brilliantly colored birds—a spectacular sight.

True and Broad-billed Rollers

The name "roller" refers to the curious rocking display flight of rollers of the genus *Coracias*: eight species of rather crowlike birds with big heads, sturdy hook-tipped bills, relatively short wings, and fairly short, weak legs and feet. They typically hunt small animals on the ground by watching and then pouncing from a perch. They may attack almost any creature from beetles to frogs and small snakes, including noxious or dangerous prey such as venomous scorpions.

These "true rollers" belong to the family Coraciidae, along with the four rollers of the genus *Eurystomus* that have shorter bills, longer wings, and even weaker legs. They are better flyers than the true rollers and hunt insects in the air rather like day-flying nightjars. Some, such as the cinnamon roller, may actually hunt alongside nightjars in the early evening. They are often known as broad-billed rollers because they have extrawide bills for scooping flying beetles and big moths out of the air and swallowing them whole.

Like the true rollers, the broad-billed species are mostly opportunist hunters, but the African cinnamon and blue-throated rollers often wait for the emergence of swarming winged termites in the late afternoon after rain and then launch a sustained mass attack. Over 200 birds may hunt together, swooping and wheeling through the huge swarms to catch up to 800 termites each within the 90 minutes or so before nightfall.

Ground-rollers

The true and broad-billed rollers have five distant, little-known relatives living in Madagascar: the ground-rollers

---

Family Coraciidae: 2 genera, 12 species

Coracias	8 species, including European roller (*C. garrulus*); racket-tailed roller (*C. spatulata*); lilac-breasted roller (*C. caudata*)
Eurystomus	4 species, eastern broad-billed roller (*E. orientalis*); azure roller (*E. azureus*); cinnamon roller (*E. glaucurus*); blue-throated roller (*E. gularis*)

Family Brachypteraciidae: 3 genera, 5 species, including:

Uratelornis	1 species, long-tailed ground-roller (*U. chimaera*)

Family Leptosomatidae: 1 species

Leptosomus	cuckoo-roller (*L. discolor*)

SEE ALSO Roller, European **15**:88; Roller, Eastern Broad-billed **18**:90; Woodpecker Family, The **18**:8; Crow Family, The **18**:90

of the family Brachypteraciidae. As the name suggests, the ground-rollers feed entirely on the ground, and unusually, they are most active at twilight. Some species, such as the long-tailed ground-roller, also nest on the ground in holes, but others nest in trees.

Cuckoo-roller

The family Leptosomatidae consists of just one species, the cuckoo-roller of Madagascar and the nearby Comoros Islands. Instead of seizing prey on the ground or snatching it out of the air, the cuckoo-roller hunts almost exclusively in the forest canopy. Its main targets are the many species of chameleons (a type of lizard) that live in the upper branches of forest trees, but it also takes insects and other small animals. Like true rollers, the cuckoo-roller nests in holes in trees, often high above the forest floor.

Common name European roller

Scientific name *Coracias garrulus*

Family Coraciidae

Order Coraciiformes

Size Length: 12–12.5 in (30.5–32 cm); wingspan: 20–22 in (51–56 cm); weight: 4.5–5.6 oz (128–159 g)

Key features Large, big-headed, short-necked, stocky crowlike bird with vivid plumage; light-blue head and underparts, rich brown back, ultramarine rump, brilliant green-blue wing coverts, flight feathers black above, violet-blue below; black bill and eye; immature duller, greener

Habits Typically hunts on ground from perch by day; migrates in large flocks

Nesting In unlined hole in large tree, cliff, or sometimes building; usually 4–5 eggs (up to 6) laid May–July; incubation 17–19 days; young fledge after 25–30 days; 1 brood

Voice Harsh, crowlike "rak-rak"

Diet Mainly large insects such as beetles and crickets; also scorpions, spiders, frogs, lizards, voles, and other small animals

Habitat Open forest, well-wooded farmland, and savanna

Distribution Southern, central, and eastern Europe, Southwest Asia, North Africa, and Africa south of the Sahara Desert

Status Declining in northwest but still abundant in eastern Europe and Africa

European Roller

Coracias garrulus

With its azure and turquoise plumage, the brightly colored European roller looks more at home in its African winter quarters than it does under the gray skies of its more northerly habitats.

BIG, BOLD, AND BEAUTIFUL, A EUROPEAN roller in summer plumage is an exotic, even startling sight. It often sits in full view on an exposed perch, glowing with brilliant, almost electric blue coloration and revealing flashes of even brighter blue as it spreads its wings to swoop down and snatch a meal from the ground.

Yet beneath the roller's striking plumage is a rather clumsy looking bird. With its big head, stocky body, short legs, and small feet it seems a little top-heavy. But most of the bird's power is concentrated in the large, hook-tipped bill, which it uses to snatch up and kill its prey.

Wide-ranging Appetite

The European roller hunts in warm, sunny open country with plenty of perches, as well as trees for nesting. Mixed farmland suits it well, as does open woodland, but in areas of dense forest it is found only at the forest edge or in clearings. Each bird claims its own hunting territory, selecting a stout perch with a good view of the ground below. Sitting alone, it watches and waits.

A roller is no specialist when it comes to prey. It will attack virtually anything that moves, provided its victim is small enough to swallow. It may pounce on any animal from a snail to a small snake, but its main targets are big, heavily armored beetles, grasshoppers, mantises, spiders, and scorpions. It shows great skill in avoiding the deadly sting of a scorpion and seems to be oblivious to the acrid taste of many insects that other birds reject as inedible. The European roller even devours caterpillars that bristle with defensive irritating hairs. Like

⊙ *Prey as large as this sand lizard pose no problems for the European roller.*

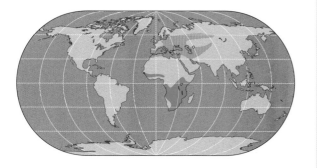

all rollers, it has a very well-developed system for dealing with indigestible material, coughing up a neat pellet of compacted hairs and insect armor every hour or so during the day.

The bird usually carries its victim back to the perch, first softening it up by crushing it in its bill or hitting it against the perch to make it easier to swallow whole. If it has caught a dangerous animal like a small venomous snake, the battering also serves to immobilize the creature before it can bite back.

Breeding in the North

European rollers pair up on their wintering grounds in the dry grasslands of Kenya, Tanzania, and Namibia before migrating north to find suitable nesting sites. The migration itself is dramatic, with hundreds of thousands of birds flying north over a narrow coastal strip of East Africa in an airborne column that stretches from one horizon to the other. They cross seas and deserts in a flight of up to 6,000 miles (9,660 km), covering an average of 68 miles (110 km) a day as they spread out across Europe and southwest Asia.

The destination of each pair is a suitable nesting hole, usually in a large tree. Over the last 30 years such sites have become increasingly scarce, however. Furthermore, the widespread use of agricultural pesticides has destroyed their food supply, causing a serious decline in the number of rollers nesting in western Europe. In Austria, for example, the breeding population decreased by 90 percent between 1970 and 1990, and European rollers have completely disappeared from Germany and Sweden.

Many are also killed on migration, especially in Oman, where local hunters armed with air rifles shoot many hundreds every spring as they pass through on their way to Europe. Luckily, the European roller still arrives in force on its African wintering grounds, so it must still be doing well in the less intensively farmed parts of its breeding range.

Eastern Broad-billed Roller

Eurystomus orientalis

Common name Eastern broad-billed roller (dollarbird)

Scientific name *Eurystomus orientalis*

Family Coraciidae

Order Coraciiformes

Size Length: 10.5–12.5 in (27–32 cm); wingspan: 20–22 in (51–56 cm); weight: 3.9–7.6 oz (111–215 g)

Key features Stocky, large-headed, long-winged roller; short, dark-red legs; shortish tail; plumage dark greenish-blue or purplish, with blackish head, blue throat, and large, oval pale silvery-blue patches on dark-blue flight feathers; short, deep, very broad scarlet bill; black eye with dark red eye ring; immature duller and darker with black-and-yellow bill

Habits Hunts in the air from a treetop perch, mainly in late afternoon and early evening; usually perches alone or in pairs, but may gather at insect swarms

Nesting In unlined tree hole; 3–5 eggs; incubation 22–23 days; chicks fledge in about 25 days; 1 brood

Voice Harsh, chattering "kek-ek-ek-ek-ek-k-k-k"

Diet Large flying insects: mainly beetles, but also crickets, cicadas, sawflies, and termites; also lizards on the ground

Habitat Woodland and forest in hot lowlands, plus farmland and open country with scattered trees

Distribution China, Japan, India, Indochina, Indonesia, New Guinea, northern and eastern Australia

Status Generally common, but rare and declining in Japan and Philippines

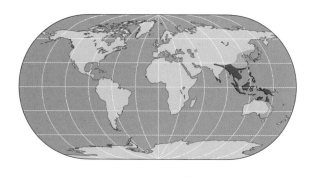

Often known as the dollarbird because of the pale, coinlike patches on its wings, the eastern broad-billed roller is a familiar sight over a vast swath of the Far East from the fringes of Siberia to the southeastern tip of Australia.

"TRUE" ROLLERS LIKE THE EUROPEAN roller (*Coracias garrulus*) are ground-attack birds that target their victims from low perches. By contrast, the broad-billed rollers of the genus *Eurystomus* are aerial hunters and operate more like flycatchers or nightjars. They select high perches such as telephone wires or exposed branches at the tops of trees and dart up to snatch flying insects out of the air. Their longer, more pointed wings give them more speed and agility in the air than *Coracias* rollers, and they also have shorter, stouter, and wider bills—ideal for seizing and swallowing insects on the wing.

Dollars on the Wing

Of the four species of broad-billed roller, the most widespread is the eastern broad-billed roller, or dollarbird. It has darker, less conspicuous plumage than a ground-hunting roller, but it is recognizable in flight by the silvery markings above and below each wing. It lives in a variety of terrain, favoring open woodland but readily colonizing forests with clearings, plantations, bamboo thickets, mangrove swamps, fields and pastures with isolated trees, and even tree-lined city streets. The bird's tolerance for disturbed and diverse habitats gives it a big advantage in the modern world and probably explains why it is still flourishing throughout most of its range.

The eastern broad-billed roller often spends much of the day perched on a high branch or wire, either alone or in pairs. It may fly up to

⊙ *An eastern broad-billed roller at its nest in New South Wales, Australia. The bird usually occupies old woodpecker or barbet holes excavated in living or dead trees.*

SEE ALSO Birds of Prey **15**:8; Nightjars and Frogmouths **15**:78; Roller, European **15**:88; Flycatchers, Old World **17**:66

snatch an insect, but mostly it sits still, moving only its head to monitor its surroundings. If defending a breeding territory, it will launch itself at other birds, driving them away with raucous calls, but then returns to its post.

Toward late afternoon the bird starts to hunt in earnest, pursuing flying beetles, bugs, crickets, and other large airborne insects with amazing agility. Wheeling and swooping over the treetops like a falcon, it seizes each victim individually and usually crushes and swallows it in flight. Occasionally a dollarbird comes down to the ground to snatch up a lizard, but apart from this it catches nearly all its prey in the air.

Any particularly big insects are taken back to the perch to be immobilized and even dismembered by shaking, tossing, and crushing. The ground below a favorite perch becomes littered with horny wings, beetle wingcases, legs, and other indigestible parts that have been deliberately broken off or dislodged by the rough treatment. Unlike true rollers, the dollarbird only rarely subdues its victim by beating it against the perch; its bill is powerful

Rock and Roll

Rollers get their name from the intimidating "rolling" display flight that many species use to defend their territory against rival males and other intruders. The most spectacular performances are put on in the breeding season by male *Coracias* rollers such as the European roller (*C. garrulus*), which hurls itself into a long, slanting dive to within a few feet of the ground while vigorously rocking its body, but not its head, from side to side several times a second. Just before hitting the ground, it swoops up to gain height and dive again. It often repeats the display several times until the intruder is driven off.

The performances of *Eurystomus* rollers can be almost as dramatic. A dollarbird defending its territory rises high in the air and dives headfirst with constant raucous calls, rolling briefly as it pulls out of the dive to climb and dive again repeatedly for several minutes. Both sexes may defend the nest site in this way, and the display is also used during courtship.

⊕ *An eastern broad-billed roller in flight. They are acrobatic birds, well able to catch insects on the wing.*

enough to deal with its victims and sufficiently broad to engulf all but the biggest prey.

Like the African broad-billed rollers (*Eurystomus glaucurus* and *E. gularis*), the dollarbird has a taste for the flying ants and termites that swarm from their nests in mass mating flights. Nonbreeding, nonterritorial birds often gather in force to exploit these events, sweeping back and forth through the swarms to snatch up as many insects as possible.

Some tropical populations of the dollarbird are resident, staying on the same territories throughout the year. They are able to do this because insects are always available. But to the north and south of the tropics the supply of insect prey drops in winter, and the birds are forced to migrate toward the equator to regions where flying insects are still abundant.

See-saw Migration

Dollarbirds that breed in China and Japan, for example, fly south to Indochina and Malaysia in September to avoid the northern winter. At the same time, the birds that have spent the southern winter in New Guinea fly south to

breed in eastern Australia. When the Australian breeders fly north again in March, the northern breeders leave the tropics to return to China and Japan. The movements have been described as "see-saw migration" because

when the northern birds move into the tropics, the southern birds move out, and vice versa.

The birds breed in isolated territorial pairs. They often reoccupy the same nest hole several years in succession and jealously defend the breeding territory against intruders until the eggs are laid. During the incubation period they lie low; but when their chicks are fledging, they become very aggressive again. It may be because the chicks demand so much food that the parent birds cannot tolerate any competition for their prey supply.

Loss of Nest sites

Like all rollers, the dollarbird needs trees for nesting; and in regions where the trees have been swept away, it has become uncommon or even rare. In Japan and the Philippines, for example, deforestation has eliminated much of the dollarbird's former breeding habitat, and it has become very scarce. Elsewhere, the bird's adaptability enables it to thrive in all kinds of unlikely habitats, and on its tropical wintering grounds it actually prefers degraded, regrown woodland to the original pristine rain forest. So provided it always has somewhere to nest, the dollarbird seems assured of a bright future.

⊙ An eastern broad-billed roller chick. The large gape that will help the bird catch flying insects when it is grown is already evident.

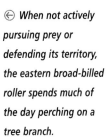

⊙ When not actively pursuing prey or defending its territory, the eastern broad-billed roller spends much of the day perching on a tree branch.

Easy Meat

Being opportunist hunters, rollers never miss a chance for an easy meal. Anything that flushes prey into the open is welcomed, and one of their most powerful allies is fire. Both aerial and ground-hunting rollers are attracted to the smoke and heat of a bushfire, often congregating in groups of 20 or more to pick off the insects escaping the flames. The birds perch as close as they dare and either snatch insects from the ground in front of the advancing fire or sally out to snatch fleeing insects from the air. In much the same way ground-feeding species like the lilac-breasted roller (*Coracias caudata*) of southern and eastern Africa associate with large grazing animals like antelope and zebra, so they can catch the insects and other animals disturbed by their feet.

The Swallow Family

Hirundinidae

Throughout the world vast numbers of insects hatch in the warmer months and take wing to find food and breeding partners. Many do not get far before they are eagerly devoured by a variety of insect-eating birds. Most of these hunters use different tactics to secure their prey, yet the sheer number of flying insects is so great that two groups of birds—the swifts and the swallows—are able to thrive using virtually the same hunting technique.

Swifts and swallows are so similar that many people have difficulty telling them apart, yet their origins are quite different. Swifts are allied to nightjars and owls, while swallows are part of the vast order of passerines, or perching birds, and are more closely related to larks and wagtails. Swifts and swallows have come to resemble each other because they live in a similar way by catching insects in the air. They have also developed similar adaptations for the same task: For example, they both have small bills with a wide gape, streamlined bodies, long pointed wings, and superb flying skills.

Swifts and swallows may be different, but swallows and martins are essentially the same. They all belong to one family, and some species are variously known as swallows and martins depending on where they are found. The American bank swallow, for example, is the same bird as the Eurasian sand martin. Of the 81 species, only two are untypical: the African river martin and the very rare white-eyed river martin of Southeast Asia. Both have unusually large bills and extrastrong feet, and are sometimes classified in a separate subfamily.

Rich Pickings

Most swallows and martins live in the tropics, and some 34 species are found only in sub-Saharan Africa. In such regions insects are available throughout the year. But there are also rich pickings in the temperate regions of the world, particularly in the continental north, where the onset of summer sees all the flying insects taking to the air at once. So several swallow species migrate north to breed each spring, flying up to 8,000 miles (12,875 km) as far as the fringes of the Arctic, and in this way they extend their range to cover most of the world.

When flying insects become scarce in late summer, the swallows and martins disappear from the northern

Family Hirundinidae: 16 genera, 81 species, including:	
Hirundo	35 species, including barn swallow (*H. rustica*); American cliff swallow (*H. pyrrhonota*); crag martin (*H. rupestris*); fairy martin (*H. ariel*)
Psalidoprocne	9 species, including Fanti sawwing (*P. obscura*); mountain sawwing (*P. fuliginosa*)
Tachycineta	8 species, including violet-green swallow (*T. thalassina*)
Progne	6 species, including purple martin (*P. subis*)
Riparia	4 species, including bank swallow or sand martin (*R. riparia*)
Delichon	3 species, including house martin (*D. urbica*)
Pseudochelidon	2 species, African river martin (*P. eurystomina*); white-eyed river martin (*P. sirintarae*)
Stelgidopteryx	2 species, including northern rough-winged swallow (*S. serripennis*)
Cheramoeca	1 species, white-backed swallow (*C. leucosterna*)

SEE ALSO Swallow, Barn **15**:96; Swallow, Bank **15**:100

skies and migrate south again. At one time they were thought to hibernate like bats, and at least one warm-temperate species, the Australian white-backed swallow, may survive short spells of bad weather by roosting in burrows and saving energy by entering a torpid state very like hibernation.

Friends and Neighbors

Swallows and martins feed almost exclusively on insects, plus the occasional airborne spider, seizing and swallowing them in flight. The bigger the bird, the bigger the prey it takes, which allows species of different sizes to hunt together without suffering too much competition for food. Eurasian house martins, for example, take small flies and aphids, while the barn swallows that often feed alongside them target larger insects like blowflies. Large American martins such as the purple martin catch and eat butterflies and even dragonflies.

All these species are familiar to us because they nest in, on, and around our houses, and in many areas they rarely nest anywhere else. The house martin originally nested on cliffs, but throughout Europe it now prefers to build its mud nests beneath the eaves of buildings or under bridges. The purple martin still nests in tree holes in western North America, but over much of its range it takes advantage of specially provided multiple nest boxes.

The birds are welcome because they devour so many insect pests. They also have other talents: Centuries ago purple martins were encouraged by the local people of what is now the southeastern U.S. because they drove away crop-raiding crows. And since all swallows and martins do well in open habitats, the clearance of forests for agriculture probably helped them expand their ranges. Yet modern intensive farming does them no favors because the demolition of old farm buildings eliminates many nesting sites, and pesticides destroy their insect prey. It is a sad but a familiar story.

⊝ The vaselike, colonial nests of fairy martins are made from pellets of mud that they collect from nearby rivers in their Australian habitat.

⊜ A male violet-green swallow from North America at its nest hole in a tree.

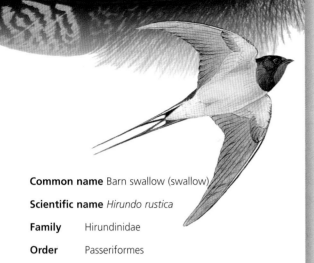

Common name Barn swallow (swallow)

Scientific name *Hirundo rustica*

Family Hirundinidae

Order Passeriformes

Size Length: 6.7–7.5 in (17–19 cm); wingspan: 12.5–13.7 in (32–35 cm); weight: 0.6–0.8 oz (17–23 g)

Key features Slim, medium-sized swallow; small bill; long wings and forked tail, with outer tail feathers elongated into streamers; shiny metallic blue-black above, pale to reddish buff below with blue-black chest band and chestnut forehead and throat; sexes similar; female has shorter tail streamers; juvenile duller, with paler forehead and throat, and short tail streamers

Habits Hunts in the air by day, mostly at low level, often over water, with graceful swooping flight; often perches on overhead wires

Nesting Open, featherlined cup of mud and dry grass on ledge, usually in outbuilding or beneath bridge, sometimes in cave or tree; 4–6 eggs; incubation 11–19 days; chicks fledge in 18–23 days; 2–3 broods

Voice Song a melodious, twittering warble; call a sharp "tswit tswit"

Diet Flying insects, particularly large flies such as blowflies, horseflies, and hoverflies

Habitat Open country, especially grassland, pasture, and marsh grazed by large animals, with suitable buildings for nesting

Distribution Temperate Eurasia and North America, Africa, Central and South America

Status Common but declining in north due to loss of breeding sites, feeding habitat, and prey

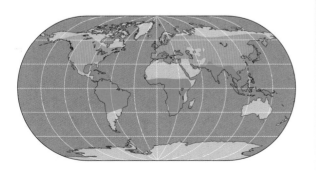

Barn Swallow

Hirundo rustica

Throughout the northern lands of the world, the annual appearance of the forktailed barn swallow is an eagerly awaited sign that the warm days of summer have finally arrived.

FAST, GRACEFUL, AND SUPREMELY AGILE in the air, with long wings and tail streamers, the barn swallow is one of the most elegant of all hunting birds. It is also one of the most successful, with a range that extends virtually worldwide apart from Australasia, the icebound polar regions, and a few oceanic islands.

Insect Diet

The barn swallow feeds almost entirely on flying insects, and like other insect-hunters, it retreats to the tropics to find prey in winter. Barn swallows from northern Europe fly 6,000 miles (9,656 km) or more to southern Africa, while North American birds make similar journeys to Latin America. In spring they return north to breed and take advantage of the seasonal flush of hatching insects to rear their young.

In the tropics the barn swallow eats a wide variety of small insects, including flying ants and aphids, but in the north the bird prefers big, burly flies such as blowflies, dung flies, and bloodsucking horseflies. These insects are particularly common on open grassland, where they feed on grazing animals and their dung, so the felling of forests and expansion of farming and ranching over the past 2,000 years or so have suited the barn swallow very well.

The barn swallow is often to be seen hunting at low level over pastures and stockyards, swooping among the cattle and sheep with a relaxed, fluid flight action, using its long tail to steer as it pursues its insect prey. Lakes and rivers are also good places to find prey, especially when bad weather drives most insects from the skies. At such times the barn swallow frequently hunts low over the water and even hovers over marginal plants looking

⊖ *The barn swallow thrives in climates ranging from the dusty prairies of North America to the damp Atlantic coasts of Europe and from the southern fringes of the arctic tundra to the plains of Africa.*

Broad-front Flyers

Many migrant birds follow well-defined routes as they travel from their breeding grounds to their winter quarters and back again. Birds of prey, in particular, often soar on thermal upcurrents to gain height for gliding, so they follow routes where such updrafts are common and avoid broad stretches of cool water. They are "narrow-front" migrants, all passing through the same air corridors.

By contrast, barn swallows migrate on a broad front. In Europe, for example, they work their way south in the early fall until they gather all along the northern shores of the Mediterranean. Then they set off across the water to north Africa in a great wave. After a break they carry on across the Sahara Desert without attempting to skirt the vast expanse of inhospitable sand. Swallows from Central Asia fly straight across the wastes of Arabia in the same way. Eventually they all arrive on the savanna grassland, where they can rest before carrying on south of the equator.

Many Nest Sites

Barn swallows breed in early summer, and the caterpillars provide vital protein for nesting birds and their young. The birds pair up as soon as they return from the tropics, and any that have bred before usually return to the same site and renew their pair-bond. The male arrives first, checks out the old nest, and may start repairing or rebuilding it. When the female arrives, she often takes over most of the task of nest building, while the male defends the site against rival swallows.

Originally barn swallows nested in tree cavities and rock crevices, but for centuries they have favored ledges and beams in outbuildings and roof spaces or under bridges and culverts. An ideal site is among the roof beams of an open-fronted cattle shelter in a traditional farmyard, offering protection from the weather, easy access, and a plentiful supply of flies. But barn swallows will also often nest in garages, porches, verandas, and other such places.

The nest is built from pellets of mud gathered by the birds in their bills, reinforced with dried grasses or straw, and lined with feathers. When the eggs hatch, the parent birds feed the hungry chicks on insects that they carry to the nest in their throats, like swifts. Swallows often raise a second or even third brood, although they may get some assistance

for flies and beetles that have settled on the leaves. When it needs a drink, the barn swallow darts across the surface of a pool and skims a mouthful of water from the surface with its lower bill. In early summer it also forages along woodland edges looking for caterpillars dangling from the trees on silken threads and seizes them on the wing.

⊕ It takes a week to build a new nest, and over 1,000 mud pellets like the ones this barn swallow has gathered in its beak are used in the construction.

① *Barn swallows are well adapted to a life in the air and even feed each other on the wing.*

Fine Feathers

To humans one of the most attractive features of the dashing barn swallow is its forked tail, in which each of the outer feathers is extended into a long, tapering streamer. It appears that humans are not the only ones to appreciate the tail. Males have longer streamers than females, and there is evidence that the males with the longest tail streamers get the opportunity to mate earlier and enjoy more breeding success. The females clearly prefer their mates with fine feathers and compete for the favors of the most eligible long-tailed suitors. Long streamers may indicate health, strength, and strong genes.

from one of the first brood, which stays on at the nest to help out with the food supply. Barn swallows can breed in their second year.

Heading South

At the end of the breeding season barn swallows leave their nests to perch in restless, noisy groups on overhead wires and to form mass night roosts as they prepare for migration. They often roost in reed beds, along with related species of swallows and martins. Such gatherings are frequently targeted by birds of prey such as the hobby, a fast-flying falcon that specializes in hunting swifts and swallows.

Older birds migrate first, blazing a trail for the younger birds that follow afterward. Swallows take long breaks as they move south, usually roosting in reed beds, and the young birds may stop off in an area for up to two weeks before resuming a journey that may last two months or more.

Decreasing Insect Prey

Barn swallows are still widespread, but they are less common than they once were, especially in regions where traditional mixed farming has been abandoned in favor of intensive, chemically assisted agriculture. Chemical pesticides kill off the birds' insect prey, and flies in particular have become harder to find. Many flies breed in animal dung, and it has become

less common as farmers have turned to artificial fertilizers and plowed up their pasture to grow crops. Suitable nesting sites are also becoming scarce as outbuildings are demolished and roof spaces are sealed up. So while the barn swallow will probably never disappear from northern skies, its appearance every spring will no longer be something that can be taken for granted.

↓ *Each nestling may eat more than 150,000 insects between hatching and fledging, so a pair with a brood of five chicks is kept very busy indeed.*

Common name Bank swallow
(sand martin)

Scientific name *Riparia riparia*

Family Hirundinidae

Order Passeriformes

Size Length: 5–5.5 in (12.7–14 cm);
wingspan: 10–11.5 in (25.5–29 cm);
weight: 0.5 oz (14 g)

Key features Small swallow with short bill; relatively
short, only slightly forked tail; sandy-brown
above, off-white below with brown breast
band; juvenile has pale feather edges, so
appears brighter

Habits Hunts almost entirely on the wing by day,
often over fresh water; perches on wires, bare
branches, and sometimes on shingle banks

Nesting Breeds in colonies, excavating nesting tunnel
near top of steep, soft, often sandy bank or
cliff; 4–6 eggs; incubation 14–15 days; young
fledge after 19 days; 2–3 broods

Voice Song a chattering twitter; call a dry chirp

Diet Small airborne insects such as mosquitoes
and mayflies; also airborne spiders

Habitat Open country, normally near water; near
suitable nesting sites in breeding season

Distribution North America and Eurasia, north to
subarctic zone; South America, Africa south
of Sahara Desert, northern India, and
Southeast Asia

Status Widespread and fairly common, but has
declined in western Eurasia owing to drought
and resulting prey shortages in African
winter quarters

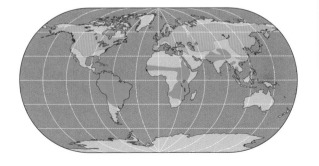

Bank Swallow *Riparia riparia*

The little bank swallow is tougher than it looks, able to fly vast distances across the globe and then use its tiny bill and feet to dig a nesting tunnel up to 15 times its own length.

IN SPRING THE BANK SWALLOW is one of the first migrants to return from its winter quarters in the tropics. The frail-looking bird often finds itself flying through a late season flurry of snow as it makes its way to its northern nesting grounds in late March. Like other swallows, the bank swallow returns to the same breeding location each year.

However, instead of finding a ready-made site in a crevice or building, the bird digs a burrow in a bank of sand or gravel. Each pair shares the bank with many others, forming a breeding colony that may number many hundreds of pairs. The bird also roosts colonially outside the breeding season, often in reed beds with other swallows and martins. There is safety in numbers, with many eyes providing early warning of deadly enemies like falcons.

Small but Effective

Also known as the sand martin, the bank swallow is the smallest and weakest of the swallows and martins. It has a fluttering, jerky flight, lacking the grace of the barn swallow (*Hirundo rustica*); but the bird is an effective hunter, able to twist and turn in the air to capture flies and other airborne prey. It feeds almost exclusively on small flying insects such as mosquitoes, midges, and mayflies. The bank swallow often hunts low over lakes, rivers, and flooded sand pits near its breeding colonies. Although the bird's bill is small, it has a very wide gape that makes an efficient insect trap.

Deep Burrowers

In the past the bank swallow usually nested in steep river banks and sandy coastal cliffs, but today it often breeds in the pits left by sand and

➔ *Bank swallows gathering at their nest site in a sandy bank. The birds often use gravel pits and other similar man-made excavations.*

⊕ *The large entrance leads to a long tunnel inclined slightly upward to allow any water to drain out easily, so keeping the nest dry.*

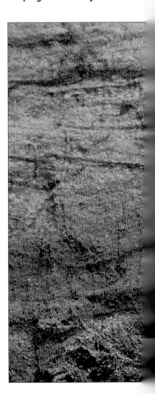

Welcome Home

When bank swallows return to their old burrows each spring, they often find them still intact; yet despite this, the birds frequently dig new burrows. They have good reason, because the old burrows are often overrun with parasites. Warm and dry, inhabited by their prey, and often reoccupied each season, the burrows make ideal homes for a variety of specialized fleas, mites, ticks, and other bloodsucking bugs.

Bank swallow fleas, for example, feed on the blood of the young birds and their parents in summer and produce huge numbers of young. They then spend the winter safely in the burrows; and when the birds return in spring, they may be met by hundreds of fleas lurking hungrily at the burrow entrance. Faced with such a reception, the swallows very naturally prefer to abandon their old home and excavate a new one.

⊕ A group of fledgling bank swallows in their nest. The nesting chamber is lined with soft grass, leaves, hair, and feathers.

times deeper depending on the nature of the material they are excavating. It can take from three days to three weeks to complete the job. When the birds are satisfied, they hollow out a nest chamber at the far end, line it with soft material, and lay their eggs.

When the eggs hatch, the colony becomes a scene of frenzied activity. With many pairs nesting in close proximity, there are always adults bringing food for their young and flying off for more. As the nestlings get bigger, they cluster at their burrow entrances to be fed, and eventually they grow their flight feathers and take to the air while their parents set about rearing another brood. Young birds are ready to breed in their second year.

Drought Victims

Toward the end of summer the young bank swallows gather in night roosts in nearby reed beds. Eventually they are joined by the older birds and often by barn swallows, forming huge roosts of up to 250,000 birds. After some days they leave for their wintering grounds in the tropics. Like other swallows, they travel slowly, stopping off for several days at a time to feed and rest; but eventually they reach the tropical grasslands of South America, Africa, northern India, and Southeast Asia. There they usually find enough insects to keep them fed until they are ready to make the long return journey the following spring.

Unfortunately, they are not always lucky. Most Eurasian bank swallows spend the northern winter in Africa on the eastern plains and on the dry Sahel zone south of the Sahara Desert. Normally these grasslands are refreshed by seasonal rains just before the swallows arrive, stimulating the growth of lush vegetation that supports swarms of insects, but in recent years these rains have shown a tendency to fail in the Sahel. One of the most severe droughts occurred in 1968. The parched land turned to dust, the plants shriveled up, the insects died or went to ground, and the bank swallows starved. The birds that escaped dying of hunger were so weakened that many fell

gravel extraction. The pits are often flooded, attracting insects that make convenient prey. Sand is ideal for burrowing, but the bank swallow has been known to tunnel into fine gravel, loamy soil, coal dust, and even heaps of sawdust near timber mills. Typically the birds pick easily worked seams high on a bank or cliff, beyond the reach of rats and weasels, and excavate strings of burrows. Although there may be a large number of burrows in a big colony, many will have been abandoned. When the birds return from migration, they inspect their old burrows carefully; and if they are uninhabitable, the bank swallows often simply dig new ones.

To do this, each bird hovers at the bank face and scrabbles with its feet to make a perch. Once it has a foothold, it starts digging in earnest, using its bill as a pick and shoveling away the loose sand with its feet. Both sexes share the work, boring the tunnel upward at a slight angle to drain any ground water that seeps through the sandy soil into the nest. The birds dig a burrow at least 12 inches (30 cm) deep, although it is often three or even six easy victim to predators. Not surprisingly, only about a quarter of the usual number of bank swallows made their way back to Europe the following spring.

There was another catastrophic drought in the Sahel in late 1983, with similar effects. Since then drought has become a chronic problem in the region—possibly caused by global climate change—and its effects have been made worse by the felling of trees for firewood and overgrazing of the remaining vegetation by domestic livestock. The denuded soil dries out and blows away, and the Sahel is slowly becoming a desert. It may not be long before the Eurasian populations of the bank swallow go into serious decline simply because they have nowhere to go in winter.

⊕ *Bank swallows gathering on a wire fence prior to their migration south to their winter quarters in the tropics. These North American birds are destined to spend the winter in South America.*

Exotic Dangers

Many bird enthusiasts become quite expert about the local habitats and feeding habits of summer visitors, yet know very little about how they live in the tropics. One consequence of this is that we tend to take their return in spring for granted and assume that any declines in numbers are caused by problems in our own backyard, such as loss of nesting sites or suitable prey.

The history of the bank swallow shows that is not always true. In Europe it has plenty of suitable nesting sites thanks to the spread of sand and gravel workings, yet its numbers have declined because its African winter habitat is being destroyed. It is not the only bird to suffer like this. In central Europe 14 of the 15 breeding species that have suffered serious declines in recent years are birds that spend the winter in tropical Africa.

For some the problem is lack of food caused by drought or habitat destruction. For others—especially migrant birds of prey—the threat is in the form of DDT-type pesticides that are still widely used in the tropics to combat disease-carrying mosquitoes. Even more birds are shot by hunters as they pass overhead on migration. For such birds the shrinking yet cherished wild places of the industrialized north may seem like welcome refuges.

The Shrike Family

Laniidae

Shrikes are handsome, often colorful songbirds with noisy calls, yet they behave more like miniature birds of prey—watching out for smaller, vulnerable animals and either pouncing on them from a perch or pursuing and catching them in flight. Notoriously, some species impale their victims on stout thorns to keep them secure while they reduce them to bite-sized pieces or to save them for eating later: a macabre habit that has earned them the alternative name of butcher birds.

Shrikes Aplenty

There are many different types of shrikes, most of them living in the tropics. Over three-quarters of all shrikes—some 48 species—spend their lives in Africa south of the Sahara Desert, and three others live in tropical Asia. But at least 11 species breed in temperate North America and Eurasia up to the edge of the Arctic. After nesting as far north as Canada and Alaska, the North American shrikes retreat south to the southern states. The shrikes that breed in northern Europe and Asia also winter in milder regions further south, and some join the tropical species on the savannas and woodlands of southern Africa and Southeast Asia. Some more southerly populations can find food on their breeding grounds throughout the year and therefore do not migrate.

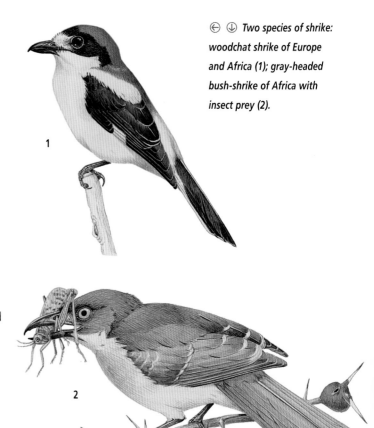

⊛ ⊕ *Two species of shrike: woodchat shrike of Europe and Africa (1); gray-headed bush-shrike of Africa with insect prey (2).*

Family Laniidae: 8 genera, 63 species

Lanius	at least 23 species, including great gray or northern shrike (*L. excubitor*); loggerhead shrike (*L. ludovicianus*); red-backed shrike (*L. collurio*); fiscal shrike (*L. collaris*); woodchat shrike (*L. senator*)
Laniarius	14 species, including crimson-breasted gonolek (*L. atrococcineus*); southern boubou (*L. ferrugineus*)
Telophorus	10 species, including four-colored bush-shrike (*T. quadricolor*); olive bush-shrike (*T. olivaceus*)
Malaconotus	6 species, including fiery-breasted bush-shrike (*M. cruentus*); gray-headed bush-shrike (*M. blanchoti*)
Dryoscopus	6 species, including black-backed puffback (*D. cubla*)
Corvinella	2 species, including yellow-billed shrike (*C. corvina*)
Lanioturdus	1 species, chat-shrike (*L. torquatus*)
Nilaus	1 species, brubru shrike (*N. afer*)

All the northern-breeding shrikes belong to one genus, *Lanius*, and are often known as "true shrikes." They are mainly black, white, and gray birds with villainous-looking black masks that suit their raptorial habits. Two of them—the great gray or northern shrike and the similar loggerhead shrike—live in North America; the great gray shrike is also widespread across Eurasia.

The strictly African shrikes are of four main types: the puffbacks, boubous, and two types of bush-shrikes. The puffbacks are similar to true shrikes, but the males have the habit of fluffing up their back feathers like powder puffs during their courtship displays. The boubous and bush-shrikes are more colorful—almost dazzlingly so in species like the fiery-breasted bush-shrike. Despite the colors, they are often hard to spot because of their skulking habits and are more easily located by their

 SEE ALSO Shrike, Red-backed **15:**108; Sparrow, House **16:**108

Dealing with Poisonous Prey

Shrikes often leave their victims impaled on thorns for some time, and that can have unexpected benefits. The North American loggerhead shrike, for example, regularly preys on slow-moving lubber grasshoppers, which defend themselves by producing a repellent foam of acrid, poisonous chemicals. They advertise their foul-tasting nature with warning stripes of black and red, and most insect-eating birds soon learn to leave these grasshoppers well alone.

But the loggerhead shrike is not so easily deterred. Seizing a grasshopper, it quickly kills it and skewers it on a spine. It then leaves the impaled corpse for at least a day. As the hours pass, the poisons in the grasshopper's body break down and lose their toxicity, allowing the shrike to eat it with no ill effects.

⊙ Some shrikes, like this great gray shrike, impale their victims on thorns or other sharp spikes (such as barbed wire) in order to store them for future use.

whistling calls. Many boubous perform a "call-and-response" duet, with the female answering the male so quickly that it sounds like the call of one bird.

Ground Attack

All shrikes have powerful hooked and notched bills adapted for killing and butchering prey, and most have strong legs and feet with sharp claws. The larger bush-shrikes and puffbacks hunt in the tree canopy, searching the foliage for insects and other small animals such as lizards; they also raid the nests of other birds to steal

their eggs. But most other species, including all the *Lanius* shrikes that migrate north to breed, specialize in attacking animals on the ground.

A great gray shrike, for example, prefers to hunt over open ground with trees and tall thornbushes that it can use as vantage points. It typically perches while watching and waiting, alert to the slightest movement on the ground below. When the bird sees a potential victim such as a large beetle, vole, or lizard, it glides down, seizes the prey, and either eats the victim right away or takes it back to the perch to kill it and dismember it with its bill.

At other times the shrike may search from the air by hovering, dart up to snatch flying insects, or pluck small birds from their perches. The closely related fiscal shrike of southern Africa regularly preys on other birds and has been known to kill caged canaries by grabbing their heads through the bars.

Impaled

A great gray shrike will often impale prey on a thorn to secure it before ripping it apart. That also allows the bird to leave the meal secure should another victim come within range. The shrike brings its latest prize back and impales that, too. And if it spots another easy target, the bird will often seize it as well. By degrees the shrike can build up a ghoulish "larder" of limp, skewered bodies.

This may be intentional hoarding, since a hunter never knows when it will eat again, especially in the far north where prey can be scarce. The great gray shrike certainly seems to plan ahead, since in frosty northern latitudes it often dismembers large prey and carefully impales each piece. They may then freeze overnight; but since the pieces are small enough to swallow whole, that does not matter. If the shrike had left the animal to freeze intact, it would be impossible to tear apart.

In warmer regions there is little point in hoarding prey because uneaten meat soon starts to decay in the heat. So a shrike that accumulates several impaled victims often eats only the choicest parts of each, leaving the

rest to be cleared up by scavengers. In Africa fewer shrikes regularly impale their prey, and at least one north–south migrant, the red-backed shrike, may abandon the habit on its tropical wintering grounds and take it up again when it returns north.

An African southern boubou attacks a snake. Unlike many shrikes that hunt from perches, the bird skulks in dense vegetation and hunts on or near the ground. Pairs stay in contact with duetting calls.

Dwindling Populations

The African yellow-billed shrike lives in family groups of five to fifteen birds. They defend a communal territory and cooperate to supply food to a single breeding female and her young. Such arrangements are unusual, however, and most shrikes breed as isolated pairs, each with their own territory. Tropical residents often defend their territory all year around, and migrants generally return to

the same territory each spring. Many *Lanius* shrikes are aggressively territorial, driving off all intruders. The great gray shrike will even attack trespassing birds of prey.

Tropical breeders often raise two or three broods of young each season, but northern migrants generally have time for only one. They may not even manage to breed at all, for in many northern regions intensive farming is making suitable nest sites, hunting habitat, and prey so hard to find that shrikes of all kinds are becoming scattered and rare.

→ *Compared with the mainly gray, black, and white shrikes of the genus Lanius, many African shrikes are vividly colored. The crimson-breasted gonolek shown here is one of many attractive-looking species.*

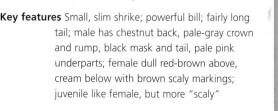

Common name Red-backed shrike

Scientific name *Lanius collurio*

Family Laniidae

Order Passeriformes

Size Length: 6.5 in (16.5 cm); wingspan: 9.5–10.5 in (24–27 cm); weight: 1 oz (28 g)

Key features Small, slim shrike; powerful bill; fairly long tail; male has chestnut back, pale-gray crown and rump, black mask and tail, pale pink underparts; female dull red-brown above, cream below with brown scaly markings; juvenile like female, but more "scaly"

Habits Normally hunts from perch by day; at other times shy and elusive

Nesting Cup nest of stalks, twigs, and debris lined with grasses, hair, and down; 5–6 eggs; incubation 13–16 days; young fledge after 14–15 days; 1 brood

Voice Song a warbling stream of mixed melodious and harsh notes, with mimicry of other birds; call a grating "schack"

Diet Mainly large insects; also lizards, rodents, and small birds

Habitat Breeds mainly in hot, dry terrain with trees and shrubs for perches; winters in savanna woodland

Distribution Europe from northern Spain to western Siberia, north to southern Scandinavia; also eastern and southern Africa

Status Declining throughout northwest Europe, probably because climate change and intensive farming are causing loss of insect prey

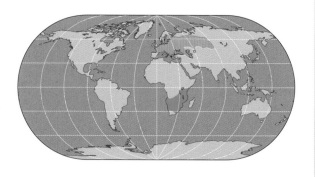

Red-backed Shrike

Lanius collurio

Although barely bigger than a sparrow, the red-backed shrike is a fierce predator ready to attack virtually any small animal within range and tear it apart with its hooked bill.

SMALL, SLIM, AND EXCITABLE, THE red-backed shrike is a ferocious bird. When defending territory, it terrorizes other birds, darting out from its perch to swoop at intruders, snapping its bill, and calling. It will readily attack birds bigger than itself, and any smaller bird that makes a slow getaway risks being killed and eaten. As a hunter it is equally determined and merciless.

Ruthless Hunter

On its northern breeding grounds the red-backed shrike favors open scrub with dense thornbushes for nesting and plenty of insect prey such as big beetles. Selecting a lookout post on top of a bush, it watches keenly for any movement on the ground below or indeed any vulnerable animal within range. The bird can target a large insect crawling over the ground from 100 feet (30 m) away, attacking in a long, shallow glide and sometimes hovering briefly before plunging in for the kill.

The shrike sometimes chases flying insects through the air, seizing them after rapid, twisting pursuits. It also pounces on larger prey such as voles, killing them with a blow to the head or neck with its powerful bill before carrying them back to the perch with its feet.

The hunting perch of a red-backed shrike can be a grisly scene because it is one of the species that regularly impales its prey on spines or barbed wire. With insects that may not be necessary; the bird can often reduce them to an edible state by beating them against the perch to dislodge their legs, wings, and wing cases. But it cannot deal with a mouse or lizard in such a way, so it skewers the animal on a barb

⊕ *A male red-backed shrike with his mouse prey impaled on a twig.*

⊙ *The male red-backed shrike (right) attracts the female (left) with excited twitterings and offerings of food, which the female receives with quivering wings and low crooning notes.*

or thorn, typically through the neck, before butchering the carcass with its hooked bill. Males are the main users of this technique, and then only in the breeding season, probably because they must catch larger prey to supply brooding females and their young.

Complicated Migration Route

Red-backed shrikes spend the northern winter on the wooded savannas of southern Africa, returning north each spring to breed. The males arrive first and claim territories by singing from exposed perches. Within a day or two the first females appear. Following courtship, the male builds the nest, which often incorporates scraps of cloth or string as well as natural materials like grass and twigs.

After breeding, red-backed shrikes return to tropical Africa, with many flying east along the northern shores of the Mediterranean before heading south to make a landfall near

⊕ *A fledgling red-backed shrike exercises its wings in the nest. The young birds are ready to breed when in their second year.*

the Nile Delta. From here they continue south down the Nile and Rift Valley to skirt the Sahara and reach the savannas of eastern and southern Africa. In spring they return north via Arabia.

Victim of Changes

A century ago red-backed shrikes routinely nested in northwestern Europe, but since then they have steadily contracted their range to the south and east. In the late 1800s, for example, they were common and widespread in Britain; but today they are scarce, and breeding is almost unknown. The long decline has probably been caused by climatic changes making the summers on the north Atlantic coast cooler, wetter, and less attractive to the large insects that are the shrike's main prey. The process has been accelerated by loss of habitat and prey caused by intensive farming—factors that are steadily driving the bird from its former breeding grounds throughout western Europe.

⊖ *The red-backed shrike's nest is usually built in dense, thorny bushes, such as the bramble shown here. During nesting males provide food while the females incubate the eggs and brood the young.*

List of Orders and Families

Birds make up the class Aves, one of the groups of vertebrate animals. The class Aves is subdivided into a number of orders and families. Listed below are the orders and families of living birds—although not all ornithologists agree on a single, standard system of classification, and therefore some differences exist in other systems. The most common names of the birds within each family are given. Where a family is described in detail, the volume or volumes in which it appears are also listed.

Order Struthioniformes
FAMILY STRUTHIONIDAE	Ostrich *Volume 11*

Order Casuariiformes
FAMILY DROMAIIDAE	Emu *Volume 11*
FAMILY CASUARIIDAE	Cassowaries *Volume 11*

Order Rheiformes
FAMILY RHEIDAE	Rheas *Volume 11*

Order Apterygiformes
FAMILY APTERYGIDAE	Kiwis *Volume 11*

Order Tinamiformes
FAMILY TINAMIDAE	Tinamous *Volume 11*

Order Galliformes
FAMILY PHASIANIDAE	Pheasants, partridges, quails, peafowl *Volume 11*
FAMILY CRACIDAE	Guans, curassows *Volume 11*
FAMILY TETRAONIDAE	Grouse *Volume 11*
FAMILY MEGAPODIIDAE	Mallee fowl, brush turkey *Volume 11*
FAMILY NUMIDIDAE	Guinea fowl *Volume 11*
FAMILY MELEAGRIDIDAE	Turkeys *Volume 11*

Order Anseriformes
FAMILY ANATIDAE	Swans, geese, ducks *Volume 12, 14*
FAMILY ANHIMIDAE	Screamers

Order Gruiformes
FAMILY OTIDIDAE	Bustards *Volume 11*
FAMILY TURNICIDAE	Button quails, quail plover *Volume 11*
FAMILY CARIAMIDAE	Seriemas *Volume 11*
FAMILY RHYNOCHETIDAE	Kagu *Volume 11*
FAMILY GRUIDAE	Cranes *Volume 14*
FAMILY ARAMIDAE	Limpkin *Volume 14*
FAMILY RALLIDAE	Rails, coots *Volume 14*
FAMILY PSOPHIIDAE	Trumpeters *Volume 19*
FAMILY MESITORNITHIDAE	Mesites
FAMILY PEDIONOMIDAE	Plains wanderer
FAMILY HELIORNITHIDAE	Sungrebes
FAMILY EURYPYGIDAE	Sunbittern

Order Piciformes
FAMILY INDICATORIDAE	Honeyguides *Volume 17*
FAMILY GALBULIDAE	Jacamars *Volume 17*
FAMILY PICIDAE	Woodpeckers, wrynecks *Volume 18*
FAMILY BUCCONIDAE	Puffbirds *Volume 19*
FAMILY CAPITONIDAE	Barbets *Volume 19*
FAMILY RAMPHASTIDAE	Toucans, aracaris *Volume 19*

Order Coraciiformes
FAMILY ALCEDINIDAE	Kingfishers *Volume 14*
FAMILY CORACIIDAE	Rollers *Volume 15*
FAMILY BRACHYPTERACIIDAE	Ground-roller *Volume 15*
FAMILY LEPTOSOMATIDAE	Cuckoo-roller *Volume 15*
FAMILY MEROPIDAE	Bee-eaters *Volume 17*
FAMILY UPUPIDAE	Hoopoe *Volume 17*
FAMILY MOMOTIDAE	Motmots *Volume 19*
FAMILY TODIDAE	Todies *Volume 19*
FAMILY BUCORVIDAE	Ground-hornbills *Volume 19*
FAMILY BUCEROTIDAE	Hornbills *Volume 19*
FAMILY PHOENICULIDAE	Wood-hoopoes

Order Trogoniformes
FAMILY TROGONIDAE	Trogons, quetzals *Volume 19*

Order Coliiformes
FAMILY COLIIDAE	Mousebirds *Volume 20*

Order Cuculiformes
FAMILY MUSOPHAGIDAE	Turacos *Volume 16*
FAMILY CUCULIDAE	Cuckoos, coucals, roadrunners *Volume 20*
FAMILY OPISTHOCOMIDAE	Hoatzin *Volume 20*

Order Psittaciformes
FAMILY PSITTACIDAE	Parrots, parakeets, lories *Volume 16, 19, 20*
FAMILY CACATUIDAE	Cockatoos, cockatiel *Volume 16, 19*

Order Apodiformes
FAMILY APODIDAE	Swifts *Volume 15*
FAMILY HEMIPROCNIDAE	Tree swifts *Volume 15*
FAMILY TROCHILIDAE	Hummingbirds *Volume 16*

Order Strigiformes
FAMILY STRIGIDAE	Typical owls *Volume 15*
FAMILY TYTONIDAE	Barn owls, bay owls *Volume 15*

Order Caprimulgiformes
FAMILY CAPRIMULGIDAE	Nightjars, poorwills *Volume 15*
FAMILY PODARGIDAE	Frogmouths *Volume 15*
FAMILY NYCTIBIIDAE	Potoos *Volume 15*
FAMILY AEGOTHELIDAE	Owlet-nightjars *Volume 15*
FAMILY STEATORNITHIDAE	Oilbird *Volume 15*

Order Columbiformes
FAMILY COLUMBIDAE	Pigeons, doves *Volume 16*

Order Charadriiformes
FAMILY GLAREOLIDAE	Pratincoles, coursers *Volume 11*
FAMILY LARIDAE	Gulls, kittiwakes *Volume 12*
FAMILY STERNIDAE	Terns *Volume 12*
FAMILY STERCORARIIDAE	Skuas, jaegers *Volume 12*
FAMILY RYNCHOPIDAE	Skimmers *Volume 12*
FAMILY ALCIDAE	Auklets, guillemots, puffins, razorbill, dovekie *Volume 12*
FAMILY CHARADRIIDAE	Plovers, lapwings, wrybill *Volume 13*
FAMILY SCOLOPACIDAE	Sandpipers, snipes, curlews, godwits, woodcocks *Volume 13*
FAMILY RECURVIROSTRIDAE	Stilts, avocets *Volume 13*
FAMILY PHALAROPODIDAE	Phalaropes *Volume 13*
FAMILY BURHINIDAE	Thick-knees, dikkops *Volume 13*
FAMILY HAEMATOPODIDAE	Oystercatchers *Volume 13*
FAMILY CHIONIDAE	Sheathbills *Volume 13*
FAMILY DROMADIDAE	Crab plover *Volume 13*
FAMILY IBIDORHYNCHIDAE	Ibisbill *Volume 13*
FAMILY JACANIDAE	Jacanas *Volume 14*
FAMILY ROSTRATULIDAE	Painted snipes *Volume 14*
FAMILY THINOCORIDAE	Seedsnipes

Order Pteroclidiformes
FAMILY PTEROCLIDIDAE	Sandgrouse *Volume 16*

Order Falconiformes

FAMILY PANDIONIDAE	Osprey *Volume 15*
FAMILY FALCONIDAE	Falcons, kestrels, caracara *Volume 15*
FAMILY ACCIPITRIDAE	Hawks, eagles, buzzards, kites, Old World vultures *Volume 15, 20*
FAMILY CATHARTIDAE	New World vultures, condors *Volume 15, 20*
FAMILY SAGITTARIIDAE	Secretary bird *Volume 15, 20*

Order Podicipediformes

FAMILY PODICIPEDIDAE	Grebes *Volume 14*

Order Pelecaniformes

FAMILY PELECANIDAE	Pelicans *Volume 12*
FAMILY SULIDAE	Boobies, gannets *Volume 12*
FAMILY PHAETHONTIDAE	Tropicbirds *Volume 12*
FAMILY PHALACROCORACIDAE	Cormorants, shags *Volume 12*
FAMILY FREGATIDAE	Frigatebirds *Volume 12*
FAMILY ANHINGIDAE	Darters

Order Ciconiiformes

FAMILY ARDEIDAE	Herons, egrets, bitterns *Volume 14*
FAMILY CICONIIDAE	Storks *Volume 14*
FAMILY THRESKIORNITHIDAE	Ibises, spoonbills *Volume 14*
FAMILY SCOPIDAE	Hamerkop
FAMILY BALAENICIPITIDAE	Shoebill *Volume 14*
FAMILY PHOENICOPTERIDAE	Flamingos *Volume 14*

Order Sphenisciformes

FAMILY SPHENISCIDAE	Penguins *Volume 12*

Order Procellariiformes

FAMILY DIOMEDEIDAE	Albatrosses *Volume 12*
FAMILY PROCELLARIIDAE	Shearwaters, fulmars, petrels *Volume 12*
FAMILY HYDROBATIDAE	Storm-petrels *Volume 12*
FAMILY PELECANOIDIDAE	Diving-petrels *Volume 12*

Order Gaviiformes

FAMILY GAVIIDAE	Loons or divers *Volume 14*

Order Passeriformes

FAMILY EURYLAIMIDAE	Broadbills *Volume 20*
FAMILY MENURIDAE	Lyrebirds *Volume 11*
FAMILY ATRICHORNITHIDAE	Scrub-birds *Volume 11*
FAMILY DENDROCOLAPTIDAE	Woodcreepers *Volume 17*
FAMILY FURNARIIDAE	Ovenbirds, earthcreepers, horneros *Volume 20*
FAMILY THAMNOPHILIDAE	Antbirds, antshrikes *Volume 19*
FAMILY FORMICARIIDAE	Antpittas, antthrushes *Volume 19*
FAMILY CONOPOPHAGIDAE	Gnateaters
FAMILY RHINOCRYPTIDAE	Tapaculos
FAMILY PIPRIDAE	Manakins *Volume 19*
FAMILY COTINGIDAE	Cotingas, fruiteaters, umbrellabirds, cocks-of-the-rock *Volume 19*
FAMILY TYRANNIDAE	Tyrant flycatchers *Volume 17*
FAMILY OXYRUNCIDAE	Sharpbill
FAMILY PHYTOTOMIDAE	Plantcutters
FAMILY PITTIDAE	Pittas *Volume 17*
FAMILY XENICIDAE	New Zealand wrens
FAMILY PHILEPITTIDAE	Asities
FAMILY ALAUDIDAE	Larks *Volume 18*
FAMILY HIRUNDINIDAE	Swallows, martins *Volume 15*
FAMILY MOTACILLIDAE	Wagtails, pipits *Volume 17*
FAMILY CAMPEPHAGIDAE	Cuckooshrikes
FAMILY PYCNONOTIDAE	Bulbuls *Volume 16*
FAMILY IRENIDAE	Leafbirds
FAMILY LANIIDAE	Shrikes *Volume 15*

FAMILY PRIONOPIDAE	Helmet shrikes
FAMILY VANGIDAE	Vanga shrikes
FAMILY BOMBYCILLIDAE	Waxwings *Volume 18*
FAMILY DULIDAE	Palmchat
FAMILY CINCLIDAE	Dippers *Volume 14*
FAMILY TROGLODYTIDAE	Wrens *Volume 17*
FAMILY MIMIDAE	Mockingbirds, thrashers, catbirds *Volume 18*
FAMILY PRUNELLIDAE	Accentors *Volume 18*
FAMILY TURDIDAE	Thrushes *Volume 18*
FAMILY TIMALIIDAE	Babblers
FAMILY SYLVIIDAE	Old World warblers *Volume 17*
FAMILY MUSCICAPIDAE	Old World flycatchers *Volume 17*
FAMILY PLATYSTEIRIDAE	Old World flycatchers *Volume 17*
FAMILY MONARCHIDAE	Old World flycatchers *Volume 17*
FAMILY ORTHONYCHIDAE	Logrunners
FAMILY ACANTHIZIDAE	Australasian warblers
FAMILY RHIPIDURIDAE	Fantail flycatchers
FAMILY PACHYCEPHALIDAE	Thickheads
FAMILY MALURIDAE	Fairy-wrens *Volume 18*
FAMILY PARADOXORNITHIDAE	Parrotbills
FAMILY PARIDAE	Tits, chickadees *Volume 17*
FAMILY AEGITHALIDAE	Long-tailed tits *Volume 17*
FAMILY REMIZIDAE	Penduline tits
FAMILY SITTIDAE	Nuthatches *Volume 18*
FAMILY CERTHIIDAE	Treecreepers *Volume 17*
FAMILY RHABDORNITHIDAE	Philippine creepers
FAMILY CLIMACTERIDAE	Australasian treecreepers
FAMILY ZOSTEROPIDAE	White-eyes *Volume 18*
FAMILY PARAMYTHIIDAE	Flock berrypeckers *Volume 18*
FAMILY DICAEIDAE	Flowerpeckers
FAMILY PARDALOTIDAE	Pardalotes
FAMILY NECTARINIIDAE	Sunbirds, spiderhunters *Volume 19*
FAMILY MELIPHAGIDAE	Honeyeaters, spinebills *Volume 20*
FAMILY EPHTHIANURIDAE	Australian chats
FAMILY EMBERIZIDAE	Buntings, New World sparrows, cardinals, Galápagos finches *Volume 16, 20*
FAMILY PARULIDAE	New World warblers *Volume 17*
FAMILY DREPANIDIDAE	Hawaiian honeycreepers *Volume 20*
FAMILY VIREONIDAE	Vireos *Volume 17*
FAMILY ICTERIDAE	New World blackbirds, orioles *Volume 18*
FAMILY FRINGILLIDAE	Finches *Volume 16*
FAMILY ESTRILDIDAE	Waxbills *Volume 16*
FAMILY PLOCEIDAE	Weavers, sparrows, queleas *Volume 16*
FAMILY STURNIDAE	Starlings, mynas *Volume 18*
FAMILY ORIOLIDAE	Orioles, figbirds
FAMILY DICRURIDAE	Drongos *Volume 17*
FAMILY CALLAEIDAE	New Zealand wattlebirds *Volume 20*
FAMILY CORCORACIDAE	Australian mudnesters *Volume 20*
FAMILY ARTAMIDAE	Woodswallows, butcherbirds *Volume 20*
FAMILY GRALLINIDAE	Magpie-larks
FAMILY CRACTICIDAE	Bell magpies
FAMILY PTILONORHYNCHIDAE	Bowerbirds *Volume 19*
FAMILY PARADISAEIDAE	Birds of paradise *Volume 19*
FAMILY CORVIDAE	Crows, magpies, jays, ravens *Volume 18*

Glossary

Words in SMALL CAPITALS refer to other entries in the glossary.

Adaptation features of an animal that adjust it to its environment. NATURAL SELECTION favors the survival of individuals whose adaptations fit them to their surroundings better than other individuals

Adaptive radiation when a group of closely related animals (e.g., members of a FAMILY) have evolved differences from each other so that they occupy different NICHES

Adult a fully grown animal that has reached breeding age

Air sac thin-walled structure connected to the lungs of birds that aids respiration

Alarm call call given to warn others of the presence of a PREDATOR

Albinism abnormally white PLUMAGE (whole or partial) caused by lack of PIGMENT; true albinos also have red eyes, pink legs, and a pink beak

Allopreening the act of one bird PREENING another

Allospecies one of the SPECIES within a SUPERSPECIES

Allula group of several small, strong FEATHERS on leading edge of WING; used in flight to reduce turbulence and prevent stalling

Altricial refers to young that stay in the NEST until they are more or less full grown (as opposed to PRECOCIAL). See also NIDICOLOUS

Anisodactyl feet with three toes pointing forward and one pointing backward

Antarctic the continent, islands, sea, and ice that surround the South Pole

Anting highly specialized behavior in which a bird uses its BILL to apply ants to the PLUMAGE or lets ants invade its plumage, apparently in order to use the ants' acidic and antibiotic secretions to protect the plumage against PARASITES, fungal infection, and bacteria

Aquatic associated with or living in water

Arboreal associated with or living in trees

Arctic the polar region north of 66° 33' N

Avian pertaining to birds

Axillary the bird's "armpit"; FEATHERS in this region are called axillaries

Barb side branch from the central shaft of a FEATHER

Barbicel one of the tiny, hooklike structures on BARBULES

Barbule side branch from the BARB of a FEATHER

Beak see BILL

Bill the two MANDIBLES with which birds gather their food

Binocular vision the ability to look at an object with both eyes simultaneously, which greatly improves the ability to judge its distance, for example

Brackish slightly salty water (e.g., as found in estuaries where fresh water and seawater mix)

Breastbone bone separating the ribs, often deeply keeled to hold the strong flight muscles; also called the STERNUM

Breeding season entire cycle of reproductive activity from courtship and pair formation (and often establishment of TERRITORY) through nesting to independence of young

Brood group of young raised simultaneously by a pair (or several) birds: single-brooded (birds make only one nesting attempt each year, although they may have a replacement CLUTCH if the first is lost); double-brooded (birds breed twice or more each year); also triple-, multiple-brooded

Brood parasitism condition in which one SPECIES lays its eggs in the NEST of another, so that the young are raised by "parents" of a different species

Brood patch featherless area on the breast, with many blood vessels close to surface allowing more effective egg INCUBATION

Burrow tunnel excavated in soil where eggs and young are kept safely

Call short sounds made by birds to indicate danger, threaten intruders, or keep a group of birds together. See also SONG

Camouflage markings on PLUMAGE that aid concealment

Canopy fairly continuous (closed) or broken (open) layer in forests produced by the intermingling of branches of trees; the crowns of some trees project above the canopy and are known as emergents

Cap area of single color on top of head, sometimes extending to neck

Captive breeding program the breeding of a SPECIES in captivity with aim of controlled release into the wild

Carrion dead animal matter used as food by scavengers

Casque bony extension of the upper MANDIBLE

Cere fleshy covering on BILL where the upper MANDIBLE meets the face

Chick term applied to a bird from HATCHING to either FLEDGING or reaching sexual maturity

CITES Convention on International Trade in Endangered Species; an agreement between nations that restricts international trade to permitted levels through licensing and administrative controls; rare animals and plants are assigned to categories

Class a taxonomic level; all birds belong to the class Aves; the main levels of taxonomic hierarchy (in descending order) are: phylum, class, ORDER, FAMILY, GENUS, SPECIES

Claw sharp, pointed growth at end of a bird's toes; in the case of a young hoatzin also on the "thumb" and "first finger" of the wings

Cloud forest montane forest in TROPICAL or SUBTROPICAL areas with frequent low cloud cover, often at CANOPY height

Clutch the eggs laid in one breeding attempt

Colony group of animals gathered together for breeding

Comb fleshy protuberance on the top of a bird's head

Communal breeder SPECIES in which more than the two birds of a pair help in raising the young. See also COOPERATIVE BREEDING

Community all the plants and animals that live together in a HABITAT

Conservation preservation of the world's biological diversity through research, HABITAT and SPECIES management, and education

Contour feather FEATHER with largely firm and flat vanes; contrasts with DOWN, which is soft and loose

Convergent evolution independent acquisition of similar characters in EVOLUTION, as opposed to the possession of similar features by virtue of descent from a common ancestor

Cooperative breeding breeding system in which parents of young are assisted in the care of young by other ADULT or SUBADULT birds

Countershading form of protective CAMOUFLAGE in which areas exposed to light (upper parts) are dark, and areas normally shaded (underparts) are light

Coverts smaller FEATHERS that cover the WINGS and overlie the base of the large FLIGHT FEATHERS

Covey collective name for groups of birds, usually game birds

Crèche gathering of young birds, especially penguins and flamingos

Crepuscular active at twilight

Crest tuft of FEATHERS on top of a bird's head that can often be raised and flattened, especially during courtship DISPLAYS

Crop a thin-walled extension of the foregut used to store food; often used to carry food to the nest

Cryptic CAMOUFLAGED and difficult to see

Dabbling picking food from near the surface of water without diving, submerging, or UPENDING

Dawn chorus the peak of bird SONG around sunrise

Deforestation process of cutting down and removing trees for timber or to create open space for activities such as growing crops and grazing animals

Dimorphic literally "two forms"; usually used as "sexually dimorphic" (i.e., the two sexes differ in color or size)

Dispersal movements of animals, often as they reach maturity, away from their previous HOME RANGE

Displacement activity animal behavior in a particular situation, often during times of frustration, anxiety, or indecision; examples in birds include pulling at grass, BEAK wiping, or food pecking

Display any fairly conspicuous pattern of behavior that conveys specific information to others, usually to members of the same species; often associated with "courtship," but also in other activities (e.g., "distraction," "ecstatic," or "threat" displays)

Diurnal active during the day. See NOCTURNAL

DNA (deoxyribonucleic acid) the substance that makes up the main part of the chromosomes of all living things; contains the genetic code that is handed down from generation to generation

Domestication process of taming and breeding animals to provide help and useful products for humans

Down insulating FEATHERS with or without a small shaft and with long, fluffy BARBS; the first feather coat of CHICKS; in ADULTS down forms a layer beneath the main feathers

Duetting coordinated bouts of singing or calling by a mated pair or family group of birds

Dump-nesting laying of eggs by one female bird in the nest of another; generally occurs between birds of the same SPECIES

Dust-bathing squatting on the ground and using the WINGS, BILL, and feet to work "dust" (sand or fine, dry soil) into the FEATHERS to help condition PLUMAGE and remove external PARASITES; also known as dusting

Ear tuft bunch of long FEATHERS on the head, especially in owls, that the bird erects when excited or alarmed, but have nothing to do with the ears or hearing

Echolocation method of navigation and food capture that uses echoes from emitted sounds to warn of objects in the animal's path

Eclipse plumage drab, CAMOUFLAGING femalelike PLUMAGE acquired by males after a MOLT in the fall, when they lose their FLIGHT FEATHERS and become flightless and vulnerable for several weeks

Ecosystem the COMMUNITY of living organisms and their environment

Endangered species a SPECIES whose POPULATION has fallen to such a low level that it is at risk of EXTINCTION

Endemic found only in one small geographical area

Evolution development of living things by gradual changes in their characteristics as a result of MUTATION; involves ADAPTIVE RADIATION and NATURAL SELECTION

Extinction complete dying out of a SPECIES

Eye patch large area of contrastingly colored PLUMAGE surrounding each eye of some birds

Eye ring ring of contrastingly colored FEATHERS around each eye

Eye spot an eyelike pattern on PLUMAGE (e.g., the eye spots on the long tail COVERTS of male peacocks); also known as ocellus (*pl*: ocelli)

Eye stripe stripe of contrastingly colored FEATHERS running through each eye of a bird; one above the eye is called a supercilium

Family either a group of closely related SPECIES (e.g., penguins) or a pair of birds and their offspring. See also CLASS

Feather unique structure found only in the PLUMAGE of birds; a typical body (CONTOUR), wing, or tail feather consists of a central shaft, or rachis, and a vane, or web, bearing many horizontal branches, or BARBS, each bearing many BARBULES arranged so that they are linked together by tiny hooks (BARBICELS) forming a smooth surface; the lower, bare end of the shaft, inserted in the skin, is called the quill

Filoplume hairlike feather with a shaft but few or no BARBS

Fledge to grow feathers; also refers to the moment of flying at the end of the NESTING PERIOD, when young birds are more or less completely feathered

Fledging period time from HATCHING to FLEDGING

Fledgling recently fledged young bird

Flight feathers large WING FEATHERS composed of PRIMARY FEATHERS and SECONDARY FEATHERS

Flightless bird bird SPECIES that permanently lacks the power of flight (e.g., ostriches, emus, rheas, kiwis, penguins, flightless cormorant); all evolved from flying birds

Flock assemblage of birds, often involved in a coordinated activity

Food chain sequence in which one organism becomes food for another, which in turn is eaten by another

Frugivore an animal that eats mostly or entirely fruit

Gape width of an animal's open mouth

Gene basic unit of heredity enabling one generation to pass on characteristics to its offspring

Genus (*pl.* **genera**) group of closely related SPECIES. See CLASS

Gizzard muscular forepart of the stomach; often used for grinding food

Gonys bulge toward tip of the lower MANDIBLE; most visible in gulls

Grassland terrain with vegetation that is dominated by grasses, with few or no trees

Gregarious tendency to congregate into groups

Gular pouch extension of the fleshy area of the lower jaw and throat

Habitat place where an animal or plant lives

Hatching emergence of a CHICK from its egg

Hatchling young bird recently emerged from the egg

Heterodactyl toe arrangement in which the first and second toes point backward, and the third and fourth toes point forward; unique to the trogons (family Trogonidae)

Hibernation becoming inactive in winter, with lowered body temperature to save energy

Hierarchy establishment of superiority and rank among groups of animals, with dominant individuals at the top and subordinates lower down; subordinates often give way to higher ranking birds when feeding; among POLYGAMOUS SPECIES dominant males may mate with all available females; also called pecking order

Home range area in which an animal normally lives

Homing ability of some birds to find their way back to a regular ROOST from great distances; most familiar in pigeons

Hybrid offspring of a mating between animals of different SPECIES

Immature a bird that has not acquired its mature PLUMAGE

Incubation the act of incubating the egg or eggs (i.e., keeping them warm so that development is possible)

Incubation period time taken for eggs to develop from the start of INCUBATION to HATCHING

Indigenous living naturally in a region; NATIVE (not an introduced SPECIES)

Insectivore an animal that feeds on insects

Introduced decribes a species that has been brought from places where it occurs naturally to places where it has not previously occurred

Iridescence a glittering "rainbow" effect of green, blue, or bronze caused by the scattering of light from microscopic ridges on a bird's FEATHERS

Irruption sudden or irregular spread of birds from their normal RANGE; usually as a consequence of a food shortage

IUCN International Union for the Conservation of Nature, responsible for assigning animals and plants to

internationally agreed categories of rarity (see table below)

Juvenile young bird that has not reached breeding age

Keel deep extension to the BREASTBONE or STERNUM of a bird to which flight muscles are anchored; absent from many FLIGHTLESS BIRDS

Kleptoparasitism stealing food gathered from other birds; a speciality of skuas and frigatebirds

Lamellae comblike structures used for filtering organisms out of water

Lek display ground where two or more male birds gather to attract females. See DISPLAY.

Life cycle cycle from egg, through CHICK and IMMATURE to ADULT, and then to egg again

Mallee scrub small, scrubby eucalyptus that covers large area of dryish country in Australia

Mandible one of the jaws of a bird that make up the BILL

Mantling threat DISPLAY, usually seen in birds of prey, in which a bird stands over prey, ruffles the mantle (neck) FEATHERS, and droops its WINGS slightly; the display is intended to ward off potential food pirates

Marine associated with or living in the sea

Mating act of copulation in which the cloacae of the two sexes touch, and sperm is released from the male; "mating" is also used as a general term for pair-formation

Melanism an excess of black PIGMENT (melanin) in the PLUMAGE

Migration the movement of animals from one part of the world to another at different times of year to reach food or find a place to breed

Mimicry imitation of one or more characteristics of a SPECIES by another for the gain of the imitator—e.g., vocal mimicry, PLUMAGE mimicry, or egg-coloration mimicry

Mobbing aggressive and often noisy demonstration by one bird against another in order to harass it; often refers to a collective demonstration of small birds against a PREDATOR

Molt replacement of old FEATHERS by new ones

Monogamous taking only a single mate at a time

Monotypic the sole member of a SPECIES' GENUS, FAMILY, ORDER, etc.

Morph a form, usually used to describe a color form when more than one exists

Mutation random changes in genetic material

Mutualism close association between two different organisms from which both benefit

Native belonging to an area; not introduced by humans

Natural selection process whereby individuals with the most appropriate ADAPTATIONS survive to produce offspring

Nest structure built or excavated by a bird or a preexisting site where eggs are laid and remain until they HATCH

Nesting period time from HATCHING to flying. See FLEDGE

Nestling a young bird in the nest

New World the Americas. See OLD WORLD

Niche part of a HABITAT occupied by a SPECIES, defined in terms of all aspects of its lifestyle (e.g., food, competitors, PREDATORS, and other resource requirements)

Nictitating membrane fold of skin, often translucent, which can be drawn across the eye to form a "third eyelid" for protection, lubrication, or cleaning

Nidicolous young birds that remain in the NEST until they can fly. See ALTRICIAL

Nidifugous young birds that leave the NEST soon after HATCHING. See PRECOCIAL

Nocturnal active at night. See DIURNAL

Nomadic wandering; having no fixed home

Oil gland organ located in the rump that secretes an oily substance used in FEATHER care during PREENING; also called uropygial gland or preen gland

Old World non-American continents. See New WORLD

Omnivore animal that eats a wide variety of foods from meat to plants

Opportunistic animal that varies its diet according to what is available

Order level of taxonomic ranking. See CLASS

Ornithologist scientist who specifically studies birds

IUCN CATEGORIES

EX **Extinct**, when there is no reasonable doubt that the last individual of a species has died.

EW **Extinct in the Wild**, when a species is known only to survive in captivity or as a naturalized population well outside the past range.

CR **Critically Endangered**, when a species is facing an extremely high risk of extinction in the wild in the immediate future.

EN **Endangered**, when a species faces a very high risk of extinction in the wild in the near future.

VU **Vulnerable**, when a species faces a high risk of extinction in the wild in the medium-term future.

LR **Lower Risk**, when a species has been evaluated and does not satisfy the criteria for CR, EN, or VU.

DD **Data Deficient**, when there is not enough information about a species to assess the risk of extinction.

NE **Not Evaluated**, species that have not been assessed by the IUCN criteria.

Pair-bond behavior that keeps a MATED pair together

Pampas grassy plains (of South America)

Pamprodactyl having all four toes directed forward or having the capability of being so directed

Parallel evolution development of similarities in separate, but related, evolutionary lineages through the operation of similar selective factors

Parasite bird laying its eggs in the nests of other SPECIES and leaving the foster parents to raise the young. See BROOD PARASITISM

Passerine strictly "sparrowlike," but normally used as a shortened form of Passeriformes, the largest ORDER of birds

Pecking order See HIERARCHY

Pellet compact mass of indigestible portions of a bird's food, such as FEATHERS, hair, bone, and scales, that is ejected through the mouth rather than as feces

Pigment substance that gives color to eggs and FEATHERS

Plankton layer of (usually) minute organisms that float near the surface of the ocean or in the air at a certain level above ground

Plumage all the FEATHERS and DOWN that cover a bird

Polyandry when a female mates with several males

Polygamy when a male mates with several females

Polygynous when a male mates with several females in one BREEDING SEASON

Polymorphic when a SPECIES occurs in two or more different forms (usually relating to color). See DIMORPHIC, MORPH

Population distinct group of animals of the same SPECIES or all the animals of that species

Prairie North American STEPPE grassland between 30° N and 55° N

Precocial young birds that leave the NEST after HATCHING. See ALTRICIAL

Predation the act of taking animals by a PREDATOR

Predator animal that kills live prey for food

Preening the act of arranging, cleaning, and otherwise maintaining the PLUMAGE using the BILL; often oil from the OIL GLAND is smeared over the plumage during this process

Prenuptial prior to breeding

Primary feather one of the large FEATHERS of the outer WING. See SECONDARY FEATHER

Promiscuous describes SPECIES in which the sexes come together for mating only and do not form lasting PAIR-BONDS

Quartering the act of flying back and forth over an area, searching it thoroughly

Race See SUBSPECIES

Rain forest TROPICAL and SUBTROPICAL forest with abundant and year-round rainfall; typically SPECIES rich and diverse

Range geographical area over which an organism is distributed

Raptor a bird of prey, usually one belonging to the ORDER Falconiformes

Ratites members of four orders of FLIGHTLESS BIRDS (ostrich, rheas, emus and cassowaries, kiwis) that lack a KEEL on the BREASTBONE

Regurgitation ejection of partly digested food (or the indigestible remains of food in a PELLET) from a bird's GIZZARD

Resident animal that stays in one area all the year around

Roost place where birds sleep

Salt gland part of the excretory system, helping eliminate excess salt, especially in seabirds

Savanna term loosely used to describe open grasslands with scattered trees and bushes, usually in warm areas

Scrape (or hollow) NEST without any nesting material where a shallow depression has been formed to hold the eggs

Scrub vegetation dominated by shrubs (woody plants usually with more than one stem); naturally occurs most often on the arid side of forest or grassland, but often artificially created by humans as a result of DEFORESTATION

Secondary feather one of the large FLIGHT FEATHERS on the inner WING

Sedentary nonmigrating. See RESIDENT

Semiarid describes a region or HABITAT that suffers from lack of water for much of the year, but less dry than a desert

Sequential molt situation in which FEATHERS (usually the WING FEATHERS) are MOLTED in order, as opposed to all at once

Siblings brothers and sisters

Simultaneous polyandry when a female MATES with two or more males and lays CLUTCHES of eggs for each to INCUBATE at the same time

Soaring gliding flight without wingbeats, typically with WINGS widespread, on currents of rising air or on wind currents sweeping upward over steep slopes or waves

Solitary living alone or undertaking tasks alone

Song series of sounds (vocalization), often composed of several or many phrases constructed of repeated elements; normally used by a male to claim a territory and attract a mate

Song flight special flight performance during which territorial SONG is produced; typical of birds occupying open HABITATS with few perches

Specialist animal whose lifestyle involves highly specialized strategems—e.g., feeding with one technique on a particular food

Species a POPULATION or series of populations that interbreed freely, but not with those of other species. See CLASS

Speculum distinctively colored group of FLIGHT FEATHERS

Spur sharp projection on the leg of some game birds; often more developed in males and used in fighting; also found on the carpal joint of some other birds

Steppe open, grassy plains, with few trees or bushes, of the central temperate zone of Eurasia or North America (PRAIRIES), characterized by low and sporadic rainfall and a wide annual temperature variation. "Cold" steppe: temperatures drop well below freezing point in winter, with rainfall concentrated in the summer or evenly distributed throughout the year; "hot" steppe: winter temperatures are higher and rainfall concentrated in winter months

Sternum See BREASTBONE

Stooping dropping rapidly from the air (usually by a RAPTOR in pursuit of prey)

Subadult no longer JUVENILE but not yet fully ADULT

Subarctic region close to the ARCTIC circle, or at high altitude, sharing many of the characteristics of an arctic environment

Suborder subdivision of an ORDER. See CLASS

Sub-Saharan all parts of Africa lying south of the Sahara Desert

Subspecies subdivision of a SPECIES that is distinguishable from the rest of that species; often called a RACE

Subtropics area just outside the TROPICS (i.e., at higher latitudes)

Successive polyandry when one female mates with two or more males during one BREEDING SEASON, producing separate CLUTCHES of eggs one at a time

Sunbathing spreading WINGS and tail and ruffling FEATHERS to expose skin and DOWN feathers to the sun; probably to assist the production of vitamins or to help remove PARASITES

Superspecies two or more SPECIES, geographically separated, of such close relationship that they form a single entity across their combined RANGES

Symbiosis when two or more SPECIES live together for their mutual benefit more successfully than either could live on its own

Syndactyl foot having two toes joined for part of their length

Syrinx vocal organ unique to birds at the division of the trachea

Tactolocation method of sensing, often to locate prey, by using touch

Taiga belt of coniferous forests (evergreen conifers such as firs, pines, and spruces) lying below the latitude of TUNDRA

Tail streamer specially elongated tail FEATHER (e.g., as seen on a swallow, tern, or tropicbird)

Talon sharp, hooked CLAWS used for grabbing, holding, and killing prey (usually refers to those of PREDATORS such as birds of prey and owls)

Temperate zone zones between latitudes 40° and 60° where the climate is variable or seasonal

Terrestrial living on land

Territorial defending an area; in birds usually refers to a bird or birds that exclude others of the same SPECIES from their living area and in which they will usually nest

Territory area that an animal or animals consider their own and defend against intruders

Thermal an area of (warm) air that rises by convection

Trachea See WINDPIPE

Tree hole any crevice or hollow in the trunk or limbs of a tree that can be used by birds for ROOSTING or NESTING

Tribe term sometimes used to group certain SPECIES or GENERA within a FAMILY. See CLASS

Tropics geographical area lying between 22.5° N and 22.5° S

Tundra open grassy or shrub-covered lands of the far north

Upending swiveling motion used by swimming WILDFOWL, immersing the head and foreparts of the body to reach submerged food

Vagrant individual bird blown off course or having migrated abnormally to reach a geographical area where its SPECIES is not normally found

Variety occasional variation in a SPECIES, not sufficiently persistent or geographically separated to form a SUBSPECIES

Vertebrate animal with a backbone (e.g., fish, amphibian, bird, or mammal)

Wader term sometimes used for "shorebird," including sandpipers, plovers, and related SPECIES; neither term is strictly accurate, since some species live neither on the shore nor by water

Wattle fleshy protuberance, usually near the base of the BILL

Wetland freshwater or saltwater marshes

Wildfowl inclusive term for geese, ducks, and swans

Windpipe tube that takes air from the mouth and nostrils to the lungs; also called the trachea

Wing the forelimb; the primary means of flight in flying birds, carrying the SECONDARY and PRIMARY FEATHERS (quills) and their smaller COVERTS

Wing patch well-defined area of color or pattern on the WING (usually the upper wing) of a bird

Wingspan measurement from tip to tip of the spread WINGS

Wing spur sharp projection at or near the bend of the WING. See SPUR

Wintering ground area where a migrant spends the nonbreeding season

Wishbone the furcula, formed by the two clavicles, or collar bones, joining the shoulders across the forepart of the STERNUM

Zygodactyl having two toes directed forward and two backward

Further Reading

General

Attenborough, D., **The Life of Birds**, BBC Books, London, U.K., 1998

Brooke, M., and Birkhead, T., **The Cambridge Encyclopedia of Ornithology**, Cambridge University Press, Cambridge, U.K., 1991

Chatterjee, S., **The Rise of Birds: 225 Million Years of Evolution**, The Johns Hopkins University Press, Baltimore, MD, 1997

Clements, J. F., **Birds of the World: A Checklist**, Ibis, Vista, CA, 2000

del Hoyo, J., Elliott, A., and Sargatal, J. (eds.), **The Handbook of the Birds of the World**, Vols. 1–7, Lynx Edicions, Barcelona, Spain, 1992–2002 (Vols. 8–16 in preparation)

Ehrlich, P. R., Dobkin, D. S., and Wheye, D., **The Birder's Handbook**, Simon & Schuster Inc., New York, NY, 1988

Elphick, C., Dunning, J. B. Jr., and Sibley, D., **The Sibley Guide to Bird Life and Behavior**, Alfred A. Knopf, New York, NY, 2001

Elphick, J. (ed.), **The Random House Atlas of Bird Migration**, Random House, New York, NY, 1995

Feduccia, A., **The Origin and Evolution of Birds**, Yale University Press, New Haven, CT, 1996

Gill, F., and Poole, A. (eds.), **The Birds of North America: Species Accounts**, American Ornithologists' Union, Washington, DC, 1992

Howard, R., and Moore, A., **A Complete Checklist of the Birds of the World** (2nd edn.), Academic Press, New York, NY, 1980

Jonsson, L., **Birds of Europe, with North Africa and the Middle East**, Helm, London, U.K., 1992

Kaplan, G., and Rogers, L. J., **Birds: Their Habits and Skills**, Allen & Unwin, Crows Nest, New South Wales, Australia, 2001

Marchant, S., and Higgins, P. J., **Handbook of Australian, New Zealand and Antarctic Birds**, Oxford University Press, Melbourne, Australia, 1990

Monroe, B. L., and Sibley, C. G., **A World Checklist of Birds**, Yale University Press, New Haven, CT, 1993

Page, J., and Morton, E.S., **Lords of the Air: The Smithsonian Book of Birds**, Smithsonian Institution Press, Washington, DC, 1989

Perrins, C. M., **Firefly Encyclopedia of Birds**, Firefly Books, Buffalo and Toronto, Canada, 2003

Perrins, C. M. (consultant-in-chief), **The Illustrated Encyclopedia of Birds**, Prentice Hall Press, New York, NY, 1990

Poole, A. F., Stettenheim, P., and Gill, F. B., **The Birds of North America**, American Ornithologists' Union/Academy of Natural Sciences, Philadelphia, PA, 1992–present

Sibley, D., **North American Bird Guide**, Alfred A. Knopf, New York, NY, 2000

Snow, D. W., and Perrins, C. M., **Birds of the Western Palearctic** (concise edn.), Oxford University Press, Oxford, U.K./New York, NY, 1998

Sziij, L., **Welty's Life of Birds** (5th edn.), Academic Press, St. Louis, MO, 2003

Specific to this volume

Ferguson-Lees, J., Christie, D., Burton, P., Franklin, K., and Mead, D., **Raptors of the World**, Christopher Helm, London, U.K., 2001

Hientzelman, D. S., **Guide to Owl Watching in North America**, Dover, New York, NY, 1992

Johnsgard, P., **Hawks, Eagles, and Falcons of North America**, Smithsonian Institution Press, Washington, DC, 1990

Johnsgard, P., **North American Owls**, Smithsonian Institution Press, Washington, DC, 2003

Ryden, H., **America's Bald Eagle**, Lyons Press, Guildford, CT, 1985

Savage, C., **Eagles of North America**, Greystone Books, Vancouver, Canada, 2000

Scholz, F., **Birds of Prey**, Stackpole Books, Mechanicsburg, PA, 1993

Smith, D. G., **Great Horned Owl**, Stackpole Books, Mechanicsburg, PA, 2002

Turner, A., **A Handbook to the Swallows and Martins of the World**, Christopher Helm, London, U.K., 1989

Useful Websites

General

http://www.aou.org
Founded in 1883, the American Ornithologists' Union is the oldest and largest organization in the New World devoted to the scientific study of birds

http://www.audubon.org
The website of the National Audubon Society includes news, avian science, product reports, and conservation work throughout America

http://www.birdlife.net
Website of the worldwide BirdLife International partnership, leading to partner organizations around the globe and to information about species

http://www.birds.cornell/edu
Cornell Laboratory of Ornithology website, leading to information about North American birds and actions you can take to study and conserve them

http://www.bsc-eoc.org/links
"Bird Links to the world" leads you to websites for many countries, detailing sites, species, books, and other information on the birds in each region

http://www.fatbirder.com
Fat Birder is a superb portal to 15,000 birding website links and has a page for every country in the world and all U.S., Canadian, and Australian states and provinces

http://www.surfbirds.com
A joint American-British website that includes breaking bird news items, articles of interest, rare bird reports, identification features, and more

Specific to this volume

http://www.owls.org
Website of the World Owl Trust, whose primary aim is to ensure the survival of all species of the world's owls

http://www.peregrinefund.org
A site containing information on many birds of prey

Picture Credits

Abbreviations A Ardea London; BCC Bruce Coleman Collection; FLPA Frank Lane Picture Agency; NHPA Natural History Photographic Agency; NPL naturepl.com; OSF Oxford Scientific Films; t = top; b = bottom; c = center; l = left; r = right

Jacket tl Stan Osolinski/OSF; tr Martin Harvey/NHPA; bl Haroldo Palo Jr./NHPA; br N.W. Harwood/Aquila; 9 John Downer/OSF; 10 Mark Hamblin/OSF; 13 Tony Allen/OSF; 15 T. Andrewartha/NPL; 16 François Gohier/A; 17 Kim Taylor/BCC; 19 Michael Freeman/BCC; 20 John Watkins/FLPA; 21 Andrey Zvoznikov/A; 22 Gordon Langsbury/BCC; 22–23 Helio & Van Ingen/NHPA; 25 Maresa Pryor/Animals Animals/OSF; 26 Judd Cooney/OSF; 27 B.K. Wheeler/Vireo; 29 Staffan Widstrand/BCC; 30 Stephen J. Krasemann/NHPA; 31, 32–33 Joe McDonald/BCC; 34–35 G.T. Andrewartha/FLPA; 36 Peter Pickford/NHPA; 37 Tony Heald/NPL; 38–39 R.J.C. Blewitt/A; 40 François Gohier/A; 41 Kenneth W. Fink/A; 42 Tui de Roy/OSF; 43 Daniel Heuclin/NHPA; 45t Michael Callan/FLPA; 45b G. Marcoaldi/Panda Photo/FLPA; 46–47, 48–49 Laurie Campbell/NHPA; 51 Brian Kenney/OSF; 52–53 Zig Leszczynski/Animals Animals/OSF; 55 David Kjaer/NPL; 56–57 Anthony & Elizabeth Bomford/A; 59 Richard Kolar/Animals Animals/OSF; 60t Richard & Julia Kemp/Survival Anglia/OSF; 60b Niall Benvie/NPL; 61 Brian Hawkes/NHPA; 62–63 Daniel & Julie Cox/OSF; 63 Thomas D. Mangelsen/NPL; 65t B. Roth/Okapia/OSF; 65b Martin Smith/FLPA; 66 Jany Sauvanet/NHPA; 68–69 Bill Paton/Survival Anglia/OSF; 73 Paolo Ficratti/OSF; 74 Dr. Derek Bromhall/OSF; 75 A.P. Barnes/NHPA; 76–77 By De Zylva/FLPA; 79 Konrad Wothe/OSF; 81 Bert & Babs Wells/OSF; 83 S. Maslowski/FLPA; 85 M. Gore/Windrush Photos; 87 Peter Blackwell/NPL; 88–89 Roland Mayr/OSF; 91 Jen & Des Bartlett/Survival Anglia/OSF; 92, 92–93 Morten Strange/NHPA; 93 A.N.T./NHPA; 94–95 Kathie Atkinson/OSF; 95 Tom Ulrich/OSF; 97 David Kjaer/NPL; 98 Alan Williams/NHPA; 99 Stephen Dalton/NHPA; 100–101 Alan Williams/NHPA; 101 Steve Knell/NPL; 102 Mike Birkhead/OSF; 103 P. Morris/A; 106–107 Alan Weaving/A; 107 Adrian Bailey/OSF; 108–109 Erich Thielscher/Okapia/OSF; 110–111 Dennis Green/Survival Anglia/OSF; 111 Steve Knell/NPL

Artists **Norman Arlott, Denys Ovenden, and Ad Cameron** with Trevor Boyer, Robert Gillmor, Peter Harrison, Sean Milne, and Ian Willis

Set Index

A **bold** number shows the volume and is followed by the relevant page numbers (eg., **15:** 8, 38).

Common names in **bold** (e.g., **bateleur**) mean that the bird has an illustrated main entry in the set. Underlined page numbers (e.g., **15:** 36–37) refer to the main entry for that bird.

Italic page numbers (e.g., **20:** *49*) point to illustrations of birds in parts of the set other than the main entry.

Page numbers in parentheses—e.g., **18:** (34)—locate information in At-a-glance boxes.

Birds with main entries in the set are indexed under their common names, alternative common names, and scientific names.